Critical Guides to Spanish Texts

48 Buero Vallejo: El concierto de San Ovidio

Critical Guides to Spanish Texts

EDITED BY J.E. VAREY AND A.D. DEYERMOND

BUERO VALLEJO

El concierto de San Ovidio

David Johnston

Lecturer in Modern Languages
University of Strathclyde

Grant & Cutler Ltd *in association with*
Tamesis Books Ltd 1990

350770

I.S.B.N. 84-599-3072-6
DEPÓSITO LEGAL: V. 1.706 - 1990

Printed in Spain by
Artes Gráficas Soler, S.A., Valencia
for
GRANT & CUTLER LTD
55-57 GREAT MARLBOROUGH STREET, LONDON, W1V 2AY

Contents

To my parents

Preface

The name Antonio Buero Vallejo is an inevitable point of reference
in any discussion of the modern Spanish stage. The 1949 première of
his first play, *Historia de una escalera*, did more than herald the
arrival of another talent. It forced the new Spanish theatre,
dominated since the end of the Civil War by the twin evils of
escapism and derivative modishness, to start to come of age, to
confront the problems of the times with a hitherto unknown degree
of honesty. On that evening of 14 October 1949, in the Teatro
Español, Madrid, a clear, independent and critical voice broke the
cultural silence symbolically proclaimed by Lorca's Bernarda Alba
thirteen years earlier. Since then, Buero has confirmed his stature not
only as the leading playwright of his generation, but also as the only
one who has had his work performed regularly, in Spain and abroad,
over the last four decades. It is the theatre of a writer who has
struggled for his voice to be heard, but who in that struggle has
sacrificed neither the moral substance nor the artistic integrity of his
work. The specific difficulties of the political and cultural climate
under which Buero has been working should be made clear. The
author's Republican involvement in the war, the dull and dogged
insistence of the censors, the limited financial resources available for
productions, the - until very recently at least - blinkered policy of the
state-sponsored theatre, are all factors which have militated against
the production of any new drama. Moreover, even since the death of
Franco, in 1975, all has not been plain sailing for Buero. Although
the première of *La doble historia del doctor Valmy*, a work written
in 1964 but refused performance in Spain until 1976, was hailed as
the primal cry of freedom of the nascent post-Francoist culture,
Buero's subsequent plays have received more mixed reviews. What
is certainly true, however, is that these plays have been well received

by the public at large, for whom they were written and for whom Buero Vallejo remains the acknowledged giant of the contemporary Spanish stage.

In April 1986 the Spanish theatre began to repay part of its debt to its most important living figure. The Teatro Español, as part of an extended homage, staged *El concierto de San Ovidio*, under the direction of Miguel Narros. The play ran successfully for over three months, confirming for public and critics alike that *El concierto de San Ovidio*, along with other works like *El tragaluz*, *El sueño de la razón* and *La fundación*, can now be considered as ripe for inclusion in the classical repertoire of the Spanish theatre.

All references to *El concierto de San Ovidio* are to *Teatro selecto* (Madrid: Escelicer, 1972), as are those to *Un soñador para un pueblo*. References to other plays by Buero are to the following editions: *En la ardiente oscuridad*, Colección Austral, 1510 (Madrid: Espasa-Calpe, 1972); *El terror inmóvil*, Cuadernos de la Cátedra de Teatro de la Universidad de Murcia, 6 (Murcia: Universidad, 1979); *Aventura en lo gris*, Colección Novelas y Cuentos, 158 (Madrid: Magisterio Español, 1974); *El tragaluz*, Colección Austral, 1496 (Madrid: Espasa-Calpe, 1970); *Llegada de los dioses* (Madrid: Cátedra, 1977); *La fundación*, Colección Austral, 1569 (Madrid: Espasa-Calpe, 1975). These references appear in the text as page number only. The italic figures in parentheses refer to numbered items in the Bibliographical Note, and are followed by a page reference. The abbreviation (Inter.) refers to a series of interviews which I had with Buero in Madrid in September 1985 and 1986.

At this point I would like to record my gratitude to Sr. Buero Vallejo for the warmth and unfailing courtesy with which he has responded to my many enquiries over the years. I am especially grateful to him for his encouragement in the preparation of this book.

Glasgow, 1987.

1 *Historical Drama*

The première of *El concierto de San Ovidio*, Buero Vallejo's thirteenth play to be performed, took place in the Teatro Goya, Madrid, on the evening of Friday, 16 November 1962, amidst the same 'extraordinaria expectación' (*6*, p.14) that one has come to associate with the appearance of any new work from the pen of Spain's foremost contemporary dramatist. The success of the opening night, described as 'un éxito en verdad clamoroso, pródigo en largas ovaciones y bravos' (*6*, p.14), was quickly proclaimed by a wave of generally favourable, in some cases fervent, reviews, and the play's artistic status confirmed in the longer term by the perhaps more considered opinions of major critics. Ricardo Doménech, for instance, views it as among Buero's best three or four works which are 'situadas en primerísimo lugar y de calidad equiparable' (*2*, p.66), and Luis Iglesias Feijoo describes it as 'un drama en que el autor resume todo lo que sabía y, llegado a un momento de plenitud creadora, pone a contribución lo mejor de sí mismo' (*20*, p.293). For Buero himself, *El concierto de San Ovidio* 'está entre las obras mías que yo más estimo, sin duda' (Inter.). The quality of the play was translated into commercial success. It enjoyed what by Madrid standards was a long run, being subsequently awarded the Premio Larra jointly with Lauro Olmo's *La camisa*. Since then, the play has been translated into five languages and performed internationally, as well as being televised both inside and outside Spain.

Much of the play's original impact in performance derived from the forbidden thrill of political protest, cleverly encoded and richly dramatized, which it provided for its audience. Moreover, the dramatic potential of the work's blind protagonist, David, drew from José María Rodero what is now acknowledged to be one of the finest performances in the history of the modern Spanish stage, one that was lent added interest, indeed poignancy, by the fact that at that time Rodero had himself recently undergone major eye surgery. Some years later Rodero was to recreate successfully the part of David before the Spanish television cameras, and in the 1986 production Juan Gea received very favourable notices for his interpretation of a David whose driving passion is at times masked by a nervous hostility. But, of course, no degree of excellence in performance or of impassioned political protest can compensate for a play which is fundamentally weak or flawed. In *El concierto de San Ovidio* a sense of dramatic experimentation ably combines with the mature consolidation of recognizably Buerian techniques to produce a play which is clearly the work of an author approaching the height of his creative powers. Indeed, the decade which followed the play saw the appearance of much of what is generally recognized to be Buero's best work.

In terms of the overall sweep of his theatre, *El concierto de San Ovidio* can be seen as both a chronological and an artistic midpoint between two key works, *En la ardiente oscuridad*, first performed in 1950, and the highly complex and polished *La fundación* (1974). These three works are concerned to depict man's one-dimensional existence in a world whose nature he cannot readily ascertain and which cruelly exploits his basic inability - and unwillingness - to assert himself in the face of his incomprehension. In both *En la ardiente oscuridad* and *El concierto de San Ovidio*, the latter being the more advanced in theme and technique, Buero uses a group of blind protagonists to provide a potent image of this metaphorical darkness in which man lives. In both of these works we find that one of the blind men, David in *El concierto de San Ovidio* and Ignacio in *En la ardiente oscuridad*, possesses a marked degree of spiritual insight. This figure of the visionary who struggles against the enormity of his blindness (hence the name David) or who burns with the desire to see and understand (the name Ignacio clearly reflects the burning element of the title of *En la ardiente oscuridad*) enables the dramatist to explore fully the double-edged nature of his metaphor, 'la ceguera voluntaria' and 'la ceguera involuntaria', the blindness that man imposes upon himself and that which is imposed upon him.

In fact, it was 'mi ya vieja adhesión al tema de la ceguera en su aspecto tanto real como simbólico', as Buero himself has put it (Inter.), which lay behind the genesis of *El concierto de San Ovidio* in the most direct sense. In March 1962 Buero's friend and critic, Enrique Pajón Mecloy, himself blind, produced the first edition of *Sirio*, a magazine dedicated to the problems of the visually handicapped, a copy of which he sent as a matter of course to the playwright. It was here that Buero was to discover his direct inspiration for the play. Reproduced in *Sirio* was an engraving which depicted the humiliation of an orchestra of blind musicians at the hands of an unscrupulous entrepreneur in the Paris of 1771.[1] Appended to this were the words of a certain Valentín Haüy, founder of the first school for the blind in 1783, who had been so outraged by the spectacle that he devoted his remaining years to the education of the blind.[2] Profoundly moved, as he later declared in a letter to Pajón Mecloy, Buero resolved to write a 'drama "pro ciegos" ', in which the relationship between the exploited blind beggars and the reformer Haüy would be made explicit (*17*, p.42). Accordingly, between April

---

[1]Buero states that two versions of the engraving exist. The one which inspired the play was originally published in Spain in the June 1960 issue of *El Correo de la Unesco*, a journal unofficially frowned upon by the Franco regime. This engraving is reproduced by Doménech in his edition of the play (*2*, p.72). The other, which is presently housed in the Musée Carnavalet in Paris, is reproduced in the special issue of *Primer Acto*, published in 1962.

[2]A potted biography of Valentín Haüy, in addition to a short history of the *Quinze Vingts*, is included in the edition of the play published by the Teatro Español (*4*, pp.217-19). The biography relates that 'un pequeño mendigo ciego, de dieciséis años, que pedía en la puerta de la iglesia de San Roque, Francisco Leseur, se convertirá en su primer discípulo. Como Leseur no podía perder sus ganancias, Haüy tenía que pagarle las horas de clase que le daba. Le enseñaba a leer con letras grabadas en trozos de madera fina. Su sistema tenía el defecto de querer sustituir, por medio del tacto y de los demás sentidos, el sentido de la vista. Un error común a los videntes. Pero su sistema se verá superado por Braille a partir de ese comienzo.' Haüy recorded his educational experiences in his *Essai sur l'éducation des aveugles*, published in 1786.

and the summer of 1962 Buero began a programme of research in
order to familiarize himself with eighteenth-century France,
concentrating especially on Michelet, Taine, D'Harmonville and
Montesquieu. At the same time he began to reach a deeper
understanding of what it meant to be blind in the eighteenth century,
chiefly through his reading of Villey and La Sizeranne, as Derek
Gagen notes (*17*, p.42), but also by close study of Diderot's *Lettre
sur les aveugles*, a work which had had a profound effect on
Valentín Haüy. The fruit of this meticulous research and this
compassionate awareness of the tragic situation of the blind in past
centuries began to take shape over the summer of 1962. By early
September *El concierto de San Ovidio* was finished.

Moreover, Buero clearly saw in this instance and at this
particular time an opportunity to develop more fully the sociopolitical aspects of the metaphor of blindness:

> Pero en el caso de *El concierto de San Ovidio*, además
> de esta conexión mía anterior de la ceguera, había
> también un no estar del todo satisfecho con *En la
> ardiente oscuridad*; a ver si me hago entender, no es que
> no estuviera satisfecho de la obra como tal materia
> dramática, pero sí pensaba que en efecto el tema tenía
> más proyección todavía de la que podía tener en aquella
> obra anterior, y que le faltaba, o bien que podía volverse
> a tocar desde este ángulo definidamente social e
> histórico, que a mí también me ha interesado a menudo.
> (Inter.)

Unlike *En la ardiente oscuridad*, in which the historical and political
implications are deliberately and necessarily unstated, *El concierto
de San Ovidio* is imbued with an overtly political awareness that is in
every way relevant to the Spain of its time. Now the visionary voices
his protest not only at the silent enigma of the universe, but also at
the lack of a collective sense of direction which characterized the
Franco regime.

That the moment was ripe for this type of radical attack on Spanish political and social life is shown by the successful run enjoyed by Lauro Olmo's *La camisa*, with its bitter denunciation of unemployment and poverty. There are several external factors which explain why Buero also felt encouraged to embark upon this more overt politicization of his theatre. In broad terms, 1962 was a watershed in post-war Spain . María Pilar Pérez-Stansfield contrasts, in strikingly Unamunian terms, the 'realidad de superficie' of a Spain slowly opening to foreign influence and investment with 'la realidad subterránea, que no se leía en los periódicos' of growing student and labour unrest (*31*, p.161). A widespread sense of social frustration was steadily being galvanized by political agitation into a new working-class consciousness and awarenesss of the class struggle, as the historians Raymond Carr and Juan Pablo Fusi have written.[3] Buero's theatre has, perhaps inevitably, been particularly sensitive and responsive to the shifting nuances of collective development, both reflecting and drawing out the ultimate meaning of what Doménech has called 'el oscuro vivir español de las últimas décadas' (*16*, p.300). Accordingly, written at a time of social and political ferment, the play's presentation and perspective are angled so that the work has a veiled relevance to the society in which it is performed. The spectators, who flocked to Buero's plays in search of images and words of protest, would in 1962 have had no difficulty in recognizing the superstructure of their own society reflected in the France of 1771 - the dominance of the church, the fundamental lack of democratic rights, the ultimate readiness of the system to resort to violence and torture in order to maintain privilege and to keep protest at bay, the expansion of the capitalist ethic under the umbrella of political absolutism. In this way, as Chapter 2 will attempt to show in more detail, *El concierto de San Ovidio* presents a cogent analysis of the monolithic Franco regime, and in doing so subtly reminds the spectators of the need to maintain a radically critical attitude towards the establishment of the time. It is by the open questioning of what is held to be sacrosanct authority -

---

[3]*Spain: Dictatorship to Democracy* (London: George Allen and Unwin, 1979), especially Chapter 7.

represented in the play by the powerful alliance of Church and
Aristocracy which controls the hospice where the blind beggars are
housed - that Buero believes an immature society can come
politically of age. The vast chain of progress that the play depicts is
set in motion, albeit unconsciously and indirectly, by David's
questioning of the Priora's view of the blind as the naturally
disinherited of the earth, a view confirmed by the established
ignorance of centuries. In a country hungry for images of its own
dispossession, the lesson of this situation, although removed in time
and space, would not be lost.

In this way, *El concierto de San Ovidio* addresses itself to the
specific problems of a particular time. It is this aspect of the play
that Eduardo Haro Tecglen chooses to stress in his review of the
1986 production in Madrid, describing it as 'un puente sobre el
tiempo'.[4] But the vast majority of reviewers in 1986 saw the work as
much more than an interesting relic of anti-Francoist culture.[5] It is a
clear mistake to seek to present the play as a simple mirror of its
times, projected backwards in history solely to fool the censor. *El
concierto de San Ovidio* is, unquestionably, social theatre, but there
is no reason why social theatre must remain tied to its time, even
though it may owe its first line of allegiance to the particular events
or attitudes of a particular time. Otherwise, how could we talk of the
universality of the theatre of socially committed writers like Ibsen,
O'Casey or Miller? The range of meanings enclosed in the dramatic
'parábola' of *El concierto de San Ovidio* is much more dynamic than
Haro Tecglen admits. Buero himself gives a clue to his broader
intentions:

Inevitablemente siempre se tiene la intención de referirse
de soslayo, y más en aquellos años, a la sociedad en que

[4]'Un puente sobre el tiempo', *El País* (28 April 1986).
[5]See, for example, the review by the highly respected José Monleón,
published in *Diario 16* (3 May 1986). This critic refers extensively to the
play's universal values, stressing its relevance to contemporary society in
general, and to 'todos los grupos que han padecido o padecen discriminación'
in particular.

estamos vivendo. Ahora, yo entiendo que ésta no es una condición circunstancial. Los paralelismos que se pueden establecer entre esta obra histórica mía y la situación española eran también paralelismos que, aunque en aquel momento circunstancialmente podían ser la manera de aludir a cosas no fáciles de aludir, también, y quizá primordialmente, me interesaban como tales paralelismos, con censura o sin ella. Es decir, por lo que la Historia tiene de actualidad mantenida o sostenida, sobre todo en ciertas etapas históricas, y sobre todo en España. La obra se escribe porque allí hay una enseñanza histórica.(Inter.)

The precise nature of this historical lesson must be clearly understood. To do that we must refer briefly to how Buero has seen his own role as a dramatist in Franco's Spain.

In an important talk given in Germany in 1979 Buero suggests that his central concern as an artist working under Francoism was one of fundamental recuperation (*12*, p.222). Above all, his theatre attempts to reassert social criticism in a system which will not brook dissent, and through that criticism to recover the legitimate social role of the individual, his active incorporation into the decision-making processes that condition society. Clearly, this focus on the acute lack of possibilities in the sociopolitical life of the country will also illuminate the lack of human possibility in the lives of ordinary Spaniards that, in the eyes of a 'vencido' of the Civil War, arises from their acceptance of their rigidly constrained social role, their 'ceguera voluntaria'. On this level, therefore, the theatre of Buero Vallejo endeavours to recover, or recreate, man's intimate world, the internal depth of conscience and consciousness which underpins the social role, and which enables man to draw out the ultimate meaning of his actions. In this way, Buero's theatre in general, and *El concierto de San Ovidio* in particular, situates the locus of the problem of man's political world in those trans-historical constants of human existence such as interpersonal relationships, the caring self and the development of personality.

The historical lesson that *El concierto de San Ovidio* contains, therefore, for the audience of 1986 no less than that of 1962, is that human life in its plenitude is inexorably tied to the individual's social potential, to future ways of being. There can be no frustrated withdrawal into subjectivity, into the pursuit of totally private concerns. All of this explains the third level of recuperation that we find in Buero's theatre. Many of his plays are fired by the need to rescue history itself, to define more clearly the historical framework in which the individual life is set and which, in a leftist ideology, lends it both significance and direction. In one way this springs directly from Buero's own personal experiences during and after the Civil War. In 1936 Buero became a member of the Communist Party (a membership which he did not renew after the war) and did not hesitate to volunteer for action to support the Republican cause. With the Nationalist victory in 1939, he was imprisoned and sentenced to death 'por adhesión a la rebelión', a bitter Orwellian lesson that those in power can twist the very fabric of history itself to suit their own purposes. Those who had fought to defend Spanish democracy were now rebels, ignominious in defeat. Buero's sentence was subsequently commuted to a total of seven years' imprisonment, but the lesson was not lost. His theatre takes upon itself the liberation of the dynamic process of history from those who seek to deny or falsify it.

This in itself is, of course, not a new concern in Spanish literature. In 1895, in *En torno al casticismo*, Miguel de Unamuno had endeavoured to define history as a living part of culture by showing the relevance of the past not only to the present, but also to the future.[6] Aware that the resistance to change which has constantly dogged Spanish historical development, and which has been enshrined as a hallowed principle of the powerful union of Church and State, derives wholly from the dead past, Unamuno sought to disentangle the true from the false, the dynamic from the static. It is in this light that we can understand the remark of the left-wing critic

---

[6]See my article (*22*) for an extended analysis of the influence of the early work of Unamuno on Buero's historical theatre.

José Monleón that 'con talante noventayochista, Buero sabe que la historia puede ser la gran enemiga de la intrahistoria' (*11*, p.28). In this piece of necessarily coded critical jargon Monleón stresses the disjunction, what we might now call perhaps the credibility gap, between the official version of events and processes, and how these events and processes are experienced in the individual life. Buero's plays, therefore, seek to re-establish the link between private biography and the greater flow of history, to highlight the role of the individual in collective affairs which had hitherto seemed closed or out of bounds to him. This is a concern particularly evident in *El concierto de San Ovidio*, as subsequent discussion will show, but it is evident even in Buero's earliest works. In *Historia de una escalera* time is presented in the same dualist manner as is history in *El concierto de San Ovidio*, that is, as it is experienced in the individual life, simultaneously the agent of and barrier to man's self-fulfilment, and time in its wider significance for the life of the community. The vital relation between what might be called private and historical time is illustrated by the extent to which the most intimate decisions of the characters, notably the failure of Fernando to marry Carmina, have vast repercussions on the community at large and across the generations.

Buero's theatre, then, seeks to enable the spectators to grasp fully the nature of their own relationship with history, highlighting in particular how they may contribute as individuals to the historical process. But first they must be convinced that history is a man-made product and not a chain of events or *force majeure* over which they may have no control. 'Vosotros sois...la Historia', one of the characters of *Aventura en lo gris* tells his companions (212), and it becomes a declared aim of Buero's theatre to reveal to man how much history he carries within himself. This is to be understood in two ways. On one level, it can be taken as a version of the classic Marxist dictum that social being, itself the product of historical forces, in turn determines individual consciousness, that man is the inheritor of the collective acts and impulses of the past. This correspondingly places upon the individual a responsibility towards the future, for in his hands lie the seeds of the creation of a new

world. The history that man carries within himself, therefore, refers
on this level to his history-making capabilities, his capacity to realize
his personal and group potential not only by appropriating the
tradition of which he is a part, but by developing and changing it.
One of the key lines of *El concierto de San Ovidio*, 'el hombre más
oscuro puede mover montañas si lo quiere' (604), spoken by
Valentín Haüy, is designed to reinforce the audience's belief in man
as creator of his own history. As Chapters 2 and 3 of this study will
show, in a system such as Franco's Spain in which the collective will
has been successfully neutralized, the vindication of man's potential
to act as a subject rather than be acted upon as a passive object is of
paramount importance. Describing his theatre as 'gafas para cegatos
que quisieran ver', Buero declares his intention to restore some
measure of historical sight to the politically blind of our time (11,
p.62).

This goal became more explicitly formalized in 1958 with the
première of *Un soñador para un pueblo*, a work which initiated a
cycle of historical plays (of which *El concierto de San Ovidio* is the
third). With *Un soñador para un pueblo* Buero Vallejo restored,
virtually at a stroke, serious historical drama to the post-Civil-War
stage. Pérez-Stansfield echoes Gonzalo Torrente Ballester's
complaint that the historical theatre produced in the two decades
since the end of the war had been artistically mediocre and
politically conformist, rarely rising above the tone of Hollywood
costume drama:

> Con el estreno, en 1958, de *Un soñador para un pueblo*,
> de Buero Vallejo, renace la tendencia histórica en el
> teatro español. Tendencia que en todas sus
> manifestaciones intentará comunicar al público ese
> sentido trágico que tanto echaba en falta Torrente
> Ballester. Otro vacío más de nuestro teatro empezaba a
> llenarse. (*31*, p.169)

Un soñador para un pueblo, a work which deals with Esquilache's
frustrated attempts to open up eighteenth-century Spain to the

invigorating ideals of the European enlightenment, was followed in 1961 by *Las Meninas*, in which Buero, skilfully drawing upon his own experience as an artist, recreates Velázquez's confrontation with the Inquisition. After *El concierto de San Ovidio* came, in 1970, *El sueño de la razón*, depicting Goya's forceful clash with the absolutism of Fernando VII. The most recent play in the cycle is *La detonación*, first performed in 1977, a complex work which traces Larra's fateful slide from optimism to despair as he struggles to force his society to confront its own moral bankruptcy.

The tension between the surface stasis of the nation and the growing waves of suppressed and silenced agitation that, as we have seen, became more acute in the later 1950s and early 60s explains why Buero began to produce this spate of history plays around this time. All but *El concierto de San Ovidio* are set in Spain, and their common purpose is to refresh collective memory by recalling conflictive and problematic moments in a national history officially held to be as inexorable and as consistent as the working out of some divine plan. But, beyond this concern with the particularities of Spanish history, the plays of this cycle in general, and *El concierto de San Ovidio* especially, are underpinned by the conviction voiced by Esquilache in *Un soñador para un pueblo*, namely that 'la historia se mueve' (245). It is a conviction that John W. Kronik describes as reflecting 'la concepción dinámica de la historia que se desarrolla en *Las Meninas* y *El concierto de San Ovidio*' (25, p.6). Each of the historical plays, as this brief summary of their respective plots may show, is concerned to reveal the tension between old and new which lies at the heart of every epoch. In *El concierto de San Ovidio* in particular, by counterposing the contemporary view of the blind as little more than useless animals - 'son como animalillos', as one member of the orchestra's audience puts it (551) - against the striving figure of David, the dramatist creates through the play a potent image of the struggle of the progressive against the reactionary in the onward march of history. Through David, Buero seeks to remind his spectators of their great humanistic and historical task, namely to create the future rather than accept it as a static destiny. David's taunt to his blind companions, paralysed by their fear, that 'estáis muertos y no lo sabéis' (490), becomes Buero's indictment of his own country of the blind.

El concierto de San Ovidio, therefore, in common with the other plays of the historical cycle, centres on this same struggle against the dead hand of official history, the liberation of the future from the tyranny of the continuing past. This is not to suggest that Buero is indulging in his own form of historical determinism, attempting to redefine the past in order to predict with certainty Spain's new radical future. *El concierto de San Ovidio* shows clearly that the future cannot be predicted on the basis of the past, emphasizing that progress is an unstable union of predictable forces and unpredictable individualism (represented respectively in the play by the French Revolution and Valentín Haüy). In this way the play attempts to wrest history from the realm of the eternal and unchanging essence of Spanishness which the Franco regime embodied, and restore human significance to it. And so we approach the synthesis of private and historical time that is the ultimate desideratum of Buero's work, lying at the heart of his philosophy of history, as Chapter 3 will show. It is at this juncture that history and ethics coincide. For Buero, the possibilities inherited from the past by the presently existing individual are to a marked extent conditioned by the conduct of those who have preceded him. To put this another way: there is a central conviction in Buero's historical theatre that the nature of man's actions and perceptions here and now determines the moral and material quality of life for future generations.

To a certain extent, this is a commonplace of the historical dramatist, but as *El concierto de San Ovidio* reveals Buero is scrupulous in portraying the collective and historical implications of the ethical stance adopted by the individual. In this sense, Buero's contention that 'las torpezas humanas *se disfrazan* de destino' (*11*, p.62) assumes key importance in the historical plays. Man's lack of faith in his capacity to change events, his failure to humanize his world, conspire to become his ultimate prison, precluding the very freedom to which he aspires. Buero's plays demonstrate this in practical terms by showing how the individual's negative actions or pessimistic perceptions create a chain of cause and effect of such proportions that it rapidly assumes the character and force of an imposed destiny. This is very much the situation in which the blind beggars find themselves at the beginning of *El concierto de San Ovidio*, as subsequent analysis will show. The intention of the play, the 'enseñanza histórica' to which Buero has referred, is to free the spectators from the destructive nexus of forces imposed from within and without ('la ceguera'), by awakening them to the clear-sighted realization that moral re-examination and correction can challenge what has been consistently presented as a static and ineluctable destiny.

This, then, is the relationship between play and spectator that Buero seeks to promote. In the specific context of the historical drama it is therefore imperative to develop a dramatic strategy which enables the spectators not only to appreciate fully the potentially liberating movement of history, but also to understand their own specific or private significance in that movement. In broad terms, *El concierto de San Ovidio* will attempt to achieve this by moving from an initial awareness of stagnation and dehumanization to a depiction of the capacity of an ordinary person to create a better future. This is the skeleton of the 'parábola' on which Buero will flesh out the rest of the play. While other dramatists made occasional attempts to root their opposition to official history's 'falsa imagen de la realidad, una imagen reiterada y retórica de la misma' (*11*, p.17) in absurdism and satire (see, for example, *El tintero*, by Carlos Muñiz, or the portrayal of officialdom in Alfonso Sastre's *Guillermo Tell tiene los ojos tristes*), Buero's historical plays set about the destruction of the myth of permanence propagated by the regime by involving the spectator in the flow of history. *El concierto de San Ovidio* certainly clarifies particular aspects of Spanish life in the early 1960s through the prism of more or less oblique historical parallels, but this mirroring realizes its full validity only with the explicitly formulated hope that nothing in the social and political world is immutable. Change is an ever-present possibility in the life of man. Pilar de la Puente writes:

Buero quiere llegar a una comprensión del pasado para
penetrar hondamente en los problemas actuales;
interpretar, desentrañados de ellos, aquello que nos
afecta como hombres de dos o tres siglos después.
Investiga en unas realidades sociales que se dieron en un
momento histórico y que por subsistir ahora o porque
algún destello del pasado revive en nuestro tiempo, son
motivos de consideración. (27, p.94)

The implications of this are important. As Pilar de la Puente
indicates, Buero's historical drama centres not on the past event nor
wholly on its significance for contemporary society, but on those
processes that develop from the past through the present into the
future. Thus, the present is illuminated not as a given reality solely to
be understood, but as a dynamic flow whose direction can be
changed. The past is inherently interesting in that it provides insights
into the unchanging elements of human psychology, but Buero's
historical plays are no mere costume dramas. They reflect the very
movement of history itself. To adapt the celebrated 'palabra en el
tiempo' of Antonio Machado, a writer greatly admired by Buero, we
can describe the history plays as 'palabra en la historia'.

     The central conflict of *El concierto de San Ovidio* illustrates
very well the dramatic strategy of the historical cycle in general. The
historical focus of the play falls on David's struggle to assert himself
in the face of exploitation and injustice. Apart from the dramatic
possibilities inherent in this confrontation between the blind
visionary and the widespread prejudice of the society of the time, the
highly emotive nature of the situation, coupled with the fact that it is
an issue by and large resolved today (by the incorporation of the
blind into everyday life) and its solution accepted as a commonplace
of our times, turns the play into a particularly appropriate illustration
of the regenerative clash between old and new. Moreover, the
spectators are shown in the clearest way that this is a clash which
takes place not solely on the level of social and political institutions,
but more importantly also in the realm of human attitudes. David's
struggle is primarily against a negative and cynical attitude of mind.

A skilful use of empathy throughout the play enables Buero to exploit the assumptions of his twentieth-century spectators, placing them firmly on the side of the revolutionary. They automatically feel David to be right, or else they must dismiss their own assumptions out of hand. In this way the spectators are encouraged to view themselves as progressive thinkers in a whole process which the play suggests to be still continuing today. This is in itself an important undermining of the possibly innate conservatism of the spectators, and a clear attack on the rigorous fear of precedent which marked the policy of the Spanish state in the Franco era.

The thematic implications of all this will occupy us in subsequent chapters. But we should not forget that we are talking about a dramatic strategy. The question of stage versus page, drama as literature or performance, is a perennial problem in theatre criticism. Buero is a writer who is thoroughly aware of the literary tradition in which he works, and his plays are imbued with a literary complexity and solidity of construction which reward the closest textual analysis. But one must always bear in mind that they are also works of theatre whose primary function is to have a specific effect on an audience. We have already seen what that effect is. How the play achieves it is our next question. The practical demands and dramatic possibilities of the stage are a major factor in any playwright's creative thinking. To understand his intentions fully, one must analyse the play as play. Indeed, Buero has always paid scrupulous attention to the formal aspects of his art, constantly striving to develop and intensify the already considerable range of his theatre. This, of course, is as it should be in the case of any major dramatist. In the context of the post-Civil-War Spanish stage there is the additional awareness on the part of the dramatist that the only valid resistance to a culture of officially-fostered banality is the creation of a quality product. In particular, Buero's cycle of historical plays initiates a movement away from the conventional realism of his earlier pieces. In *Un soñador para un pueblo* and subsequent works scenic space is used in a more complex and stylized way than had hitherto been Buero's practice. In addition, we find the introduction of Brechtian elements, although always used circumspectly and never as part of any wholesale importation of Brechtian theory. There was much in Brecht's 'epic' theatre which attracted Buero as he turned his attention to an analysis of Spanish history. The German writer's radical approach to drama was geared towards galvanizing the spectators into a critical attitude towards their social and political reality. Brecht's work is always concerned to depict man not as a fixed point, but as a process. Like Buero's historical theatre, epic theatre fixes its eyes not 'on the finish' but rather 'on the course'.[7] This had practical implications for the use Brecht made of the stage. The play is emphasized as a dynamic theatrical experience, to be assessed critically, rather than a real-life situation with which one can identify emotionally. This is precisely the point at which Buero parts company from Brecht, since he has always contended that critical analysis and emotional involvement are not necessarily incompatible activities, and that the spectator can be - and should ideally be - led to experience both reactions.[8] Consequently, Buero never attempts to alienate his spectator from the action to the extent that all empathy is ruled out. Indeed, as we have already seen, spectator/character empathy has an important part to play in Buero's overall dramatic strategy.

In *El concierto de San Ovidio*, as with the other plays of the history cycle, the stage is fully acknowledged as stage. In brief terms, the set emphasizes the play as spectacle, the action moving between clearly delimited areas. The action of the first act is divided between the Hospicio de los Quince Veintes, home of the blind beggars, and the richly appointed suite of the impresario, Valindin. The starkly functional appearance of the Hospicio, suggested sparingly and simply by curtains, contrasts sharply with Valindin's room - 'el saloncito de un burgués acomodado' (492), as the stage directions carefully indicate -, thereby creating a palpable sense of

---

[7]See Brecht's essay 'The Modern Theatre is the Epic Theatre', included in *Brecht on Theatre*, trans. John Willett (London: Eyre Methuen, 1979), pp.39-42.

[8]For a fuller treatment of this central difference between the theatres of Buero and Brecht, see Buero's own essay, 'A propósito de Brecht', *Insula*, no. 200-01 (July-August 1963), 1 and 14.

tension between these two opposed worlds. The second act, which is described as following on without interval, opens with the beggars seated on steps in front of dark curtains which subsequently pull back to reveal the 'barraca', Valindin's fairground café where the blind musicians are to perform. It is here that the scene which forms the turning-point of the play, for audience and characters alike, will take place. Accordingly, the set for this key scene is described in great detail, clearly drawn from the engraving which had inspired the play. The short second act, its dramatic impact heightened by only the briefest of pauses which separates it from the first act, parallels the scenic disposition of the preceding action; in both cases we move from the gloomy world of the blind beggars to the more lavish realm of the impresario in which carefully noted details visibly abound. In this way, the beggars are ejected bodily from the grey and insipid world, in which they may at least find a measure of security, into a world explicitly designed for the sighted, and in which the blind are vulnerable, open to exploitation. The precarious nature of the blind men's physical presence in these two areas is explicitly stressed. In the first act, in Valindin's house, the impresario is careful to warn 'cuidad de no romperme nada con vuestros palos' (500), an early indication as well of his overriding materialism, and in the café, in Act II, the beggars are anxious to appear at ease in this unfamiliar environment. '¿Subimos y bajamos bien? ¿No vacila nadie?', one of them asks Adriana, Valindin's mistress (527). In terms of the tension between light and dark, the central metaphor of Buero's theatre as a whole, this switch from a realm of comforting shadow to the glaring world in which the wretchedness of the blind is laid bare prepares the way for the scene in which David takes advantage of total darkness to kill Valindin. We sense a gradual reversal of roles between David and Valindin throughout the play, as David's clear moral superiority over his adversary translates itself increasingly into a more active control. It is a reversal we are prepared for. Valadin's central weakness of character, both symbolized and compensated for by his excessive drinking, is spelt out virtually from the beginning of the play. Conversely, David's strength of character is evident from his first appearance, and his growing confidence is

illustrated in his boast to Adriana that 'conozco el camino mejor que
tú. Puedo andarlo sin luz' (519). He makes Valindin look foolish
when he jabs his foot with his stick, and later in the third act it is
only by extreme physical force and the threat of a 'carta secreta' (a
lettre de cachet, or letter of detention), that Valindin can restore his
authority. David's final victory over Valindin is both moral
(symbolized by his winning the love of Adriana) and physical (the
killing). In this final scene the reversal of roles is complete. In the
darkness David can move freely, whereas Valindin is trapped by his
dependence on light. As Luciano García Lorenzo notes, 'el
explotador Valindin pasará en el drama de una seguridad total en sí
mismo a la impotencia más absoluta y que le llevará a la muerte' (26,
p.99). The David/Valindin conflict, the fundamental axis of dramatic
tension in the play, is therefore reinforced for the spectator by the
constant tension between light and dark which, in the case of *El
concierto de San Ovidio*, becomes more than a literary metaphor. It
marks the field of experience of characters and audience alike.

The fundamental goal of the historical drama of Buero, that is
to remind the spectators that they have a moral responsibility to
renew and maintain the struggles towards liberation undertaken in
the past, is clearly exemplified by the performance scene which
brings the second act to a close. Here the real audience becomes an
extension of the stage audience, an identification which is
strengthened by Valindin who addresses his introductory harangue to
the entire theatre (546). Furthermore, the real audience, like the stage
audience, may be inclined to laugh at the carefully engineered
grotesque appearance and songs of what Valindin calls 'la
maravillosa orquestina de los ciegos' (548). In this way, Buero
chooses to remind his public that the accepted norms of that time,
and by extension of any time, may well be unjust and inhumane.
Accordingly, to avoid the embarrassment of identifying with those
whom history has proved to be wrong, and whose cruelty is made
manifest by Haüy's outburst, the spectators of the play are nudged
into assuming a greater degree of awareness than the stage audience,
their eighteenth-century counterparts. The use of the word
'embarrassment' in this context is not accidental. Aware that a

spectator reacts both individually and as part of a group, the dramatist can manipulate both the positive and the negative reactions of his audience. The spectator who laughs at the sorry spectacle of the exploitation of the weak will probably feel ashamed when the indignant Haüy rises to his feet and, perhaps more tellingly, at the end of the play when he or she is characterized among those who 'nunca han sentido las dulces emociones de la sensibilidad' (603). Buero clearly does not go to the outrageous lengths of the Theatre of Aggression, but he does not hesitate to try to shame the unfeeling spectator in front of his fellows. Valindin's proud words, pronounced earlier in the second act, serve to remind the audience of the ultimate seriousness of their purpose:

> ¡Todos nos reímos de todos; el mundo es una gran feria!
> ¡Y yo soy empresario y sé lo que quieren! ¡Enanos,
> tontos, ciegos, tullidos! ¡Pues a dárselo! (543)

The morality of much contemporary entertainment is not so civilized or humane that these words hold no lesson for any audience in the latter half of the twentieth century. Moreover, in a society where distracting and soporific entertainments are totally at odds with the underlying realities of injustice and oppression, Buero is suggesting that laughter can often be the last refuge of the scoundrel.

Any final act is traditionally concerned to draw out the consequences, explicit and implicit, of the previous action. Although by now Buero was tending to favour the division of his plays into two parts, he returns here to the more conventional three-act form, in great part to accentuate the importance and impact of the performance scene. As the play approaches the climax of its explicit storyline, that is the relationship between Valindin, David and Adriana, the major areas of action are used in a dynamic way that steps up the dramatic rhythm of the work. As the pace quickens, the multifaceted set permits Buero to establish a tension between the street and the enclosed world of the bourgeoisie that parallels the opposition between the world of the blind beggars and that of the impresario. David has two crucial conversations with Lefranc and,

particularly, Bernier who, in the street, permit themselves to voice
the discontent that was widespread in the France of the time. David's
thoughtful reply to Bernier, '¡cuántas cosas necesitan remedio!'
(577), marks his commitment to action on a personal level, and his
method of killing Valindin in darkness is a direct consequence of
Bernier's observation that 'esta noche no hay luna' (577). But more
than this, David's words come to stand as the collective impulse
towards revolution, as subsequent analysis will show. In this way,
the multifaceted set enables the dramatist to strengthen his thematic
presentation of the two forces, one established and opulent, the other
popular and deprived, which clashed in the French Revolution.
However this dramatic tension, which exists on both a personal and
an historical level, is deliberately abated in the play's final scene, or
epilogue, by the 'palabra . . . sencilla y serena' (603) of Valentín
Haüy. This final moment of reflection, in which the character is lit
by a single spotlight, follows on immediately from the arrest of
David, but is in fact separated from it by a time lapse of thirty years.
The scene suggests a marked Brechtian influence as the character
draws out the moral implications of the play's actions, and some
critics have been quick to point this out. Nevertheless, Buero adheres
to a strictly realistic principle by having Haüy read from his own
work and ponder aloud, rather than directly address the audience.
Indeed, Buero emphasizes this point when he makes Haüy declare
'cuando no me ve nadie, como ahora . . .' (605). The effect of this
scene, as Chapter 4 will show, is clearly meant to be cathartic.

   In practical terms, for the spectators to appreciate fully the
relevance of the play to their times, it becomes vital that the
presentation of the historical material be filtered through the
contemporary artistic sensibility of the playwright. He must strike a
balance between respect for the type of historical authenticity that
characterizes the *Episodios nacionales* of Galdós or some of Ramón
J. Sender's historical novels, and his own desire to shape his material
in order to underline its wider significance. In this way, he will avoid
the twin dangers of producing a kind of costumed agitprop theatre,
relentlessly didactic or corrective, or of presenting an excessively
detached and academic vision. Thus, the historical plays of Buero

Vallejo are a blend of carefully researched fact and intuition, of documented motive and imputation, of what incontrovertibly was and what might, or should, have been. Buero has detailed the facts of history which he felt necessary to change:

> En *El concierto de San Ovidio* . . . hay alteraciones funcionales de lo que sucedió realmente. La orquestina de ciegos estuvo formado por diez músicos, y yo los reduje a seis. Que el Hospicio de los Quince Veintes, institución histórica donde vivieron los ciegos que participaron en aquella orquestina, estuviera regido por monjas es un riguroso embuste mío, porque el Hospicio estaba regido por personal civil bajo el patrocinio del Limosnero Mayor del rey de Francia. Pero me convenía, por razones de eficacia dramática y de significado, que quienes regían el Hospicio fueran monjas. Propiamente hablando estos errores no son defectos, puesto que son premeditados. (*12*, pp.225-26)

These functional changes, therefore, are part of the selective shaping of the past so that its lessons for contemporary society can be more clearly elucidated. Both Doménech (*16*, pp.204-06) and Iglesias Feijoo (*20*, pp.295-96) deal exhaustively with the factual elements on which the play relies. Briefly, the central event of the play, that is the humiliation of the blind beggars, and the character of Valentín Haüy are historically verifiable. Indeed, much of Haüy's final speech is a close translation of his actual writings, and, as I have mentioned, Buero makes use of these writings to add realism to his final scene. This final speech is divided into four parts, and the two stage directions 'Lee' signify an accurate translation from Haüy's original French. The directions 'Levanta la vista' indicate Buero's own words, what we might call his poetic recreation of Haüy's character. Certain other details in the play, the verses recited by Valindin at the opening of the concert, the existence of Melania de Salignac, the use of the 'cartas secretas', are all historically accurate. Everything else, notably the characterization of David, Adriana and Valindin, and the carefully differentiated beggars, is Buero's own creation. This is important, because it is in the trilateral relationship which occupies the greater part of the play that we can expect to see Buero's view of how the broad forces which drove the *ancien régime* into the abyss of revolution make themselves felt in the life of the individual. Once again we are concerned with the point of intersection between the individual's existence in history, with the respective responsibilities and limitations that this supposes, and what I have termed the trans-historical constants of human life, the desires, aspirations and fears which are common to all human beings of all times. This is a point to which I shall have cause to return at various moments during the course of this study.

This cleverly contrived balance between accuracy of historical focus and the intuitive angling of perspective is reflected in the play's use of language. Clearly, the linguistic pitch of any play will have a deep effect on the way that an audience responds to the work. Although Buero has produced plays rich in dramatic experiment-ation, he is a playwright who has revealed considerable caution in his use of language. One does not find in his work either the poetic exuberance of Lorca or the intense realism of Olmo. Despite the variety of settings that he has employed in his theatre, Buero has displayed little interest in developing within each play a linguistic register wholly appropriate to the subject, preferring instead to work within a similar framework of language each time. The result is a linguistic usage that is distinctly Buerian. This works particularly well in *El concierto de San Ovidio*. In this play the language must prove familiar, and yet slightly dated, to the audience. Accordingly, Buero adopts a technique similar to what George Steiner, writing about the theory of literary translation, terms 'elucidative strangeness'.[9] By introducing deliberate archaisms into an essentially

---

[9]*After Babel* (London: Oxford University Press, 1976), p.393. This form of dramatic language has also been adopted by Antonio Gala, perhaps most successfully in *Anillos para una dama*, first performed in 1973. In the prologue to this play (Colección Escena, 31 (Madrid: Ediciones M.K, 1982), p.9) Gala notes that the language used 'es de hoy, lo entendemos, pero tiene no sé qué aroma ajeno al lenguaje estrictamente de hoy'.

modern and free use of language, Buero aims simultaneously to engage and distance the spectator, to underline both the historical nature and the contemporary relevance of the action. Just as the use of 'elucidative strangeness' in the translation of a Spanish novel into English conveys to the reader unfamiliar perceptions or experiences through unusual linguistic forms, so the language of *El concierto de San Ovidio* seeks to immerse its spectator in one epoch without losing sight of the other. The most notable archaic usage in the play is the 'vos' form, which is employed to good effect in the burgeoning relationship between David and Adriana, but Doménech notes other examples (2, p.76).

The central strategy of *El concierto de San Ovidio*, based on Buero's concern for the individual and his precarious existence in history, directs the appeal of the play not solely to any class consciousness, although this is an important element, but, beyond that, to all human beings attempting to develop their own faculties and possibilities. By the exposition of a dynamic consciousness (David, Haüy) that runs counter to the static and imposed consciousness of the majority (Valindin, the Priora, the other blind beggars), the play seeks to challenge the monopoly of the status quo to set limits to human potential, to define what is possible. The ultimate goal of all of the history plays of Buero Vallejo is to create in the spectator a new consciousness, born from the struggle against history itself, which can stand against the limitations imposed by circumstances and participate actively not solely in the creation of one's life, but in the construction of one's world. In this way, Buero hopes that his spectators can assume their moral duty as human beings responsible to future generations. Jean-Paul Borel asserts that man must 'realizar lo imposible bajo la pena de ver triunfar lo inhumano, pues es este deber lo que constituye lo humano' (29, p.280). In a sense, *El concierto de San Ovidio* focuses on this struggle against historical impossibility. Let us see how history raises barriers which stand between man and his self-realization.

2 *The Denials of the Past*

Antonio Buero Vallejo is probably more of a public figure in Spain than are the leading British playwrights in this country. Frequent media exposure has ensured that his name is firmly imprinted upon the public consciousness, and his opinion is sought on all matters from Spanish politics to the possibility of extending the opening hours of shops. This of course does not imply a deep familiarity with Buero's theatre, and indeed the commonly held image of him is that of an 'amargado por su misma biografía', as a recent interviewer put it to him.[10] In one way, of course, as Buero himself has been careful to point out, this image of an embittered and destructive Buero was one fostered by Francoism in an attempt to invalidate the voice of protest that his theatre consistently raised during the years of the dictatorship. Moreover, it is also true that a merely superficial acquaintance with Buero's work will almost inevitably lead one to fix upon the dramatist's rigorously honest presentation of the destructive nexus of forces which conspires against personal and collective development. Buero's determination not to falsify human reality or to minimize the complex problems we face in the latter half of the twentieth century leads him to create moods of black despair in many scenes of his plays.

A typical moment in this respect occurs in *Llegada de los dioses*, a work first performed in 1971. Like Juan Pablo Castel of Ernesto Sábato's *El túnel*, the protagonist of this play, Julio, is an artist alienated by his unflinchingly honest vision of life. The tunnel of alienation in which Castel is trapped is translated into the specific

---

[10]José Luis Vicente Mosquete, 'Jornada de reflexión: Antonio Buero Vallejo, sonrisas y lágrimas', in the special supplement *Regreso a Buero Vallejo*, published by *El Público* in April 1986 to coincide with the production of *El concierto de San Ovidio* in the Teatro Español.

terms of Buero's theatre by the fact that Julio suffers from a psychosomatic form of blindness, the metaphorical equivalent of his emotional and intellectual blackness. In a crucial scene he attempts to rouse the teenage Nuria from the 'ceguera azul' (262) of her childhood faith in the goodness of the world. His ominous remarks about the imminence of nuclear disaster, ecological decay and human hypocrisy are designed to force her to confront the monstrous lie of innocence imposed upon her by a world of vested interests:

> No quiero hacerte daño. Lo que quiero es luchar contra el daño que te están haciendo. Pero si no puedes soportarlo, olvida y vuelve a tus juegos infantiles. (Otra pausa, entrecortada por los gemidos de NURIA.) Tú has querido que te hablase como a una mujer. . . (262)

The emotional impact of the scene intensifies as naive optimism is shattered under the onslaught of a knowing and worldly cynicism. Julio's blindness comes thereby to represent the stark despair of the individual who senses that, in the words of Edward Bond, 'the dreams of the old enlightenment have been lost'.[11] But the metaphor also denotes a limitation in the character. Like Lorca's New York, Julio is imperfect in his despair precisely because despair precludes the possibilities of real life. He remains trapped in radical withdrawal, his nihilistic gloom justifying his incapacity for action. But for Buero the truth of life cannot lie in inaction, no matter how paralyzing our perceptions may be. One of the characters of *La fundación* states the issue succinctly:

> Duda cuanto quieras, pero no dejes de actuar. No podemos despreciar las pequeñas libertades engañosas que anhelamos aunque nos conduzcan a otra prisión. (240)

---

[11]'Introduction', *The Fool' and 'We Come to the River'* (London: Methuen, 1976), p.xi.

Once again we return here to Borel's idea of the struggle against the impossible in which man must engage if he is to restore any measure of human significance to his world. Accordingly, *Llegada de los dioses* attempts to transmit to its audience a lasting image not of despair but of exhortation. The final words of the play, '¡Moriremos caminando!' (342), represent the desire of Julio's lover, Verónica, to persuade him not to allow his pessimism to blind him to the need for action in life. In a sense, '¡Moriremos caminando!' represents Buero's contribution to what Gagen has termed his participation in 'the post-Nietzschean "debate between pessimistic and optimistic vision" ' (*17*, p.41). It is a phrase which recognizes the overwhelming odds stacked against the possibilities of human fulfilment but which also refuses to be crushed into despair by that awareness. Seen in these terms, it clearly embodies the tragic hope which lies at the heart of Buero's work, namely that man's exposure to the negative side of life can strengthen his resolve, through a process of cathartic purification, to seek and create solutions.

Thus, the theatre of Buero Vallejo is a quest for truth about man and his society that is pursued through the purgative process of radical negation. Buero's procedure is markedly dialectical in this respect. What this means here is that his plays show how progress may arise from conflict; in personal terms, doubt may lead to affirmation, and, in historical terms, struggle can result in a bettering of social and political conditions. Hegel expressed this idea in a more idealistic manner, but the notion of strength gleaned from the open-eyed confrontation with despair is clearly central to his words:

> The life of the mind only attains its truth when discovering itself in absolute desolation. It achieves the power not as a positive which turns away from the negative, but only when looking the negative in the face, dwelling upon it.[12]

---

[12]G.W.F. Hegel, *Philosophy of Mind*, quoted by Moray McGowan, 'Botho Strauss and Franz Xaver Kroetz: Two Contemporary Views of the Subject', *Strathclyde Modern Language Studies*, 5 (1985), 59-75, at pp.64-65.

At this point, we must focus on the social implications of this, postponing the personal and metaphysical aspects until we come to consider Buero's theory of tragedy in Chapter 4.

Accordingly, the purpose of this chapter is to look at *El concierto de San Ovidio* in terms of its lucid presentation of a set of conditions hostile to human fulfilment, but always bearing in mind that this does not represent the entirety of response that the dramatist seeks to draw from his audience. Aware that the Panglossian semblance of social health - the notion that this might indeed be the best of all possible worlds - which was beginning to flourish in the early 1960s must be punctured if the dispossessed of society are ever to awaken to their real potential, Buero resolves in *El concierto de San Ovidio* to depict, as never before in his theatre, the bleak existence of the individual in this society. In doing so, he adopts the tactics of Julio, attempting to force a society, which he described in 1964 as 'menor de edad tanto material como espiritualmente' (*9*, p.20), to face facts, to grow up. What Buero is demanding of his society, therefore, is a greater consciousness, in the first place, of the problems to be confronted. Clearly, this can be at least partially construed as a reaction to the Francoists' profession of optimism as a pretext for simply carrying on as before. The myth of happiness must be burst so that the individual can move to a new consciousness of strength. *El concierto de San Ovidio* shows that this is a long and difficult path, but the only one if human beings do not wish to abandon their future.

Thus it is that the play seeks to speak directly about the very limited existence of the ordinary Spaniard of 1962. But, in doing so, it also allies itself with those contemporary social commentators, like Herbert Marcuse, who have laid increasing stress on the feelings of entrapment and impotence which lie at the heart of Western man's experience in the second half of the twentieth century. Living in an age when value has been supplanted by power, human beings have come to doubt their capacity to determine either their individual or social destiny, a pessimism heightened but not created by the threat of nuclear destruction. Many writers, among whom we may clearly include Buero Vallejo, have shown how the impersonal changes effected on a global scale in our social structures, man's all-powerful capacity for inhumanity to his fellows, the pervasive reality of social injustice and exploitation, are all elements which contribute to this sense of being an object at the mercy of vast forces. While for many this reduced status may not be felt to be a problem, as it clearly absolves them of any responsibility for actively contributing to the creation of either their own lives or those of others, the conscious individual begins to feel helpless against formative social pressures. It is as if history itself is out of his control, and the determinant factors of the future are running counter to his own interests and aspirations. *El concierto de San Ovidio* addresses itself to both these reactions, resignation and despair, through the central metaphor of blindness, as we shall see.

In many ways a direct descendant of the Generation of 1898, and in common with other artists and thinkers of the post-Civil War period, Buero comes to view blind hopelessness, or *abulia*, as one of the central causes of national decadence, on one hand, and of personal disintegration, on the other. This *abulia* is most insidious when it produces a feeling of hopeless inertia in the face of a given reality. It is the basic reaction off which political manipulation feeds, as the whole situation of *El concierto de San Ovidio* emphasizes. This is why, as Chapter 1 pointed out, historical faith is for Buero a vital element in both the psychological make-up of the individual and future well-being not just of Spain, but of the whole Western world which is sinking slowly into stagnation and inertia. The individual and collective implications of this lack of faith, this pessimism, are presented forcefully in *El concierto de San Ovidio*. In many ways the picture that Buero gives of contemporary man, through the blind beggars, coincides with the alienated creature that the American sociologist C. Wright Mills presents in his seminal study *The Sociological Imagination*. Describing a world in which the very shaping of history seems beyond men's grasp, Wright Mills asks:

> Is it any wonder that ordinary men feel that they cannot cope with the larger worlds with which they are so suddenly confronted? That they cannot understand the

> meaning of their epoch for their own lives? That - in
> defence of selfhood - they become morally insensible,
> trying to remain altogether private men? Is it any wonder
> that they come to be possessed by a sense of the trap?[13]

This sense of the trap, although perhaps not consciously understood
as such by many people, explains much of the listless frustration
which lies at the centre of contemporary man's experience. It is also
the basic experience of the blind beggars of *El concierto de San
Ovidio*, and through these characters Buero portrays the negative
consequences that this condition entails both for mankind's progress
through history and for the individual's sense of self. The link
between these two defining realities of human existence (in a non-
religious vision), the public and personal, the historical and the
private, the collective and the individual, forms the central axis
around which the play revolves. The beggars, unable to perceive any
possible role for themselves in the wider world, are condemned to a
life circumscribed by, and immersed in, private despair. This is what
Borel has in mind when he notes in his essay 'Teatro y política' that
'la "enfermedad social" no es sencillamente "una situación en la que
estamos", algo, muy molesto por cierto que nos sucede, sino la
privación de una parte de nosotros' (26, p.44).

    El concierto de San Ovidio illustrates the basically Marxist
notion that every individual finds himself with a given social identity
which has imposed upon it the broad limitations of an inherited
historical consciousness. It is this historical consciousness which, in
turn, dictates the limits of his or her potential development. Thus it is
that our historical awareness (in the sense of our belief, or lack of it,
in the individual's capacity to influence the wider course of events) is
directly related to the issues of authentic and inauthentic existence.
In Buero's theatre, the concept of authenticity, or plenitude, is tied to
the individual's possibilities of becoming, to the better ways of being
towards which he must strive if his world, personal and social, is not
to founder in stagnation. It will have become clear by now that
Buero's view of man, what we might call the existential dimension of

---

[13]*The Sociological Imagination* (Harmondsworth: Penguin, 1977), p.11.

his work, like that of Heidegger, has a clearly delineated temporal axis. Man exists in the present moment, indebted to the past and oriented towards the future. The moral quality of man's choices and decisions in the present will bear directly upon the type of future that awaits him and his successors (once again, we must stress the all-important link between the personal and the collective), as the case of Valentín Haüy is patently meant to show. In sharp contrast, the blind beggars are unable to contribute meaningfully to the creation of a better life for themselves, or even to experience themselves as free and active beings. This is the primary significance of their blindness. No less than Julio they represent those who are blind both to society's potential for change and to their own personal potential for creative, or authentic, life, for being a subject who determines his own actions rather than an object at the mercy of the schemes of the powerful. But rather than the victims of a paralyzing lucidity, as is obviously the case of the intellectual Julio, the blind beggars represent the vast majority of ordinary people who are reduced to the status of objects, in some cases consentingly, by the anonymous and exploitative system in which they live. The personal problem becomes the political one. It is one of reification, alienation to the degree that the individual only experiences himself as an object among other objects.

This is fundamentally an existential grasp of history. In other words, *El concierto de San Ovidio* presents the predicament of specific men whose struggle is with history itself. History is of interest in this play not in terms of great events or famous men, but in terms of the consciousness we inherit from the past. The blind beggars of *El concierto de San Ovidio* are not indebted to the past and oriented towards the future, but rather are enslaved by the dead hand of reactionary values and divorced from their potential for future development. This presentation of the human subject reduced to the status of object is underpinned by a clear analysis of specific political and conceptual structures which combine to give the audience a powerful image of an alienated society. These structures have been identified in various critical studies. The most influential is Doménech's, in which he talks of the play in terms of political oppression/liberation and class exploitation/struggle, conflicts closely related to the situation of Spain at that time (*16*, pp.204-21). Most critics have chosen to follow this line. Recently, however, Barry Jordan has seen the play as fundamentally a critique of the power structures of patriarchy, in which social and sexual identity are subjugated by the striving male ethos of an exploitative society (*23*, pp.431-50). There is perhaps one other way in which we can understand the alienation of the blind beggars, one which is related to the whole question of patriarchy identified by Jordan.

Many feminist writers complain that the historical domination of what they see as male values has tended to obscure and deform any specifically female tradition, thereby creating the impression that the very flow of life itself is male-directed. They are describing a state of cultural dispossession which is in every way relevant to the situation in which we first meet the blind beggars in *El concierto de San Ovidio*. In this case, the past has been appropriated by the dominant power-block of the sighted: 'a eso nos han condenado los que ven: han hecho el mundo para ellos', complains Nazario (486). In this way, the blind have been left devoid of any tradition in which they can recognize their own values and from which they can develop. To a certain extent this situation reflects the alienation of any marginal group. But there is also a direct relevance to the position of Buero himself, as a 'vencido' of the Civil War, taking his place along with millions of others in a Spain not of their making and whose official past, present and future they could only feel to be the creation of other people. Buero himself has recognized that his status as a 'vencido' is a factor underlying the writing of *El concierto de San Ovidio*:

> Indudablemente he sido un vencido de la guerra civil, y esto está actuando siempre en las cosas que escribo. De modo que, probablemente, en *El concierto de San Ovidio* también habrá algo de eso. Pero, si lo hay, será, digo yo, de la manera como yo he vivido mi propia derrota. Es decir, como una derrota que no lo es, porque David es también derrotado hasta el extremo mayor,

puesto que lo matan; pero es un hombre que no ha
bajado la guardia, que no ha arriado su propia bandera.
De modo que el vencido que hay dentro de mí es un
vencido que ha podido tener sus amarguras y sus
desalientos por el hecho de la derrota que le ha tocado
vivir, pero esto no le ha llevado a un abandono o a un
descreimiento de determinadas esperanzas. Y por lo
tanto creo que David puede, en cierto modo, reflejar mi
estado anímico de vencido. (Inter.)

This final phrase, 'estado anímico de vencido', a version of
'moriremos caminando', could well serve to describe the overall
effect that the play is geared to have on its audience, as my previous
discussion has been concerned to show.

These then are the various structures and causes of alienation
which Buero detects in his analysis of the concrete problems of these
particular human beings living at a particular moment. None of these
structures forms in isolation what we might call the dramatic axis of
the play, and it is important not to over-emphasize one particular
aspect at the expense of others. The dramatic core of *El concierto de
San Ovidio* coincides with the pivotal point of its author's philosophy
of history, that is the tension between the inherited possibilities open
to the individual and the authentic choices and decisions that one can
make in the light of them. As I have mentioned, this is a deeply felt
personal tension in Buero's own life, a result of direct experience in
Franco's Spain. But it should be no less clear that the blind beggars
are much more than a representation of a peculiarly Spanish
pessimism. Rather, they symbolize the one-dimensional life of
Western man, marooned between past and future, unable to find
anything in the past which gives his present existence meaning, and
unable to believe in a future which inspires any hope.

The first scene in which the beggars appear, therefore, is
designed to underline forcibly the apparent hopelessness of their
position in life. The immediate impact on the spectator is to be one
of corporate despair, of a collective lack of direction. The stage-
directions carefully state that, when the beggars appear, 'al pronto,

no es fácil distinguirlos' (481). Buero develops this point. It is precisely what these men have in common as blind people - 'sus ojos sin vida, la cortedad de sus movimientos' - and as beggars - 'las ropas seglares que, si bien diferentes, se parecen entre sí por lo humildes y maltrechas' (481)- which makes them different as a group. Therefore, it is upon these collective characteristics that the spectator will invariably fasten his early attention. Later on, of course, the demands of drama will require some sort of differentiation between the men, and Buero prepares the ground for this eventual individuation by stating that 'una observación más detenida permite advertir lo distintos que son' (481). But, at least initially, it is enough that these men come across as an image of collective dispossession, of 'seres inferiores y marginados', as Doménech has put it (*16*, p.216).

The physical blindness of the beggars is immediately associated with the aura of despair which emanates from them. Even before their first appearance on stage they are described as 'torpes' (476) and 'pobrecitos' (477), a description reinforced in the audience's mind by their slow, laborious entrance and the Priora's warning of 'cuidado.Ya conocéis el escalón' (480). The mould of fear in which the lives of these wretches have been cast becomes immediately apparent. In the words of Wright Mills, they are totally caught up in the sense of the trap. Elías's sorrowful recognition that 'no servimos para nada' (487) is a direct result of a sterile past, and Nazario's outburst 'Hermanos, ¿qué hacemos aquí desde hace siglos? ¡Reventar poco a poco!' (486) reveals a sense of stagnation which is both personal and collective. The world of these men is hermetically sealed, held in isolation both in time and space. This is what Verdú de Gregorio means when he notes that 'no existe una dialéctica ideológica entre su circunstancia [la de los ciegos] y la de sus explotadores' (*28*, p.112). Totally cut off from all sources of power, all of which are in the hands of 'los que ven' (489), these men can get no grip on life. Their only venture into the outside world is 'para que ofrezcan oraciones por las calles' (477) or to beg alms by scratching out basic tunes on their violins, and if they marry at all it can only be with 'las hermanas del pabellón de mujeres' (486). The system denies them access on all fronts to a more normal life.

Thus it is that the fearful reaction of the beggars to the plan put to them on Valindin's behalf by the Priora springs from their total inability to find any common ground with the sighted and their world. In this case the problem comes to be, how does one take the first firm step in a quicksand? Past and future merge in an image of relentlessly continuing mediocrity:

ELIAS: ¡Nunca hubo orquestas de ciegos!

LUCAS: ¡Ni las habrá! (487)

It is perhaps opportune to recall that in this type of exchange Buero is skilfully manipulating the reactions of his contemporary audience, exploiting their assumptions and awareness. The contrast with the present-day situation of the blind is acute, and so the spectator should have little difficulty in interpreting the physical blindness of these men as a sort of lack of historical faith, with all the ingrained sense of hopelessness for the present moment that this implies. Lucas's declaration of 'no future', to use a term popularized during the wave of nihilistic gloom which swept through many European cultures during the late 1970s, when contrasted with present-day achievement, serves to remind the audience that change in the affairs of man is an ever-present possibility, that pessimism is a form of blindness.

Why then do the blind beggars agree to fall in with Valindin's project, in spite of their deeply-rooted suspicions about the world of the sighted? It should be clear from the start that, no matter what David himself might think, his impassioned pleas have had little influence on their decision. In a perceptive analysis of *En la ardiente oscuridad* Pajón Mecloy gives us an important clue when he notes that the blind students of this earlier work are imprisoned within 'el agnosticismo kantiano que no admite el acceso a las metas, a las ideas' (26 p.241). In other words, the realm of interest of the beggars is rooted in the solely material. Borrowing from the terms of the celebrated dilemma which Erich Fromm sees as lying at the heart of contemporary human beings' experience, we can say that the blind beggars have no freedom to be. They can only seek to have.[14] In this there is no romanticization in Buero's depiction of the oppressed. Their level of consciousness is rigidly dictated by their tremendously restricted social being. All of course except David, whose capacity to think and plan beyond the pressure of immediate circumstances is the mark of the hero, as Chapter 3 will show. But the audience can see quite clearly that the rest of these men are the blind of history. Moreover, they have been blinded by history. As they move out from the sterile and wounding pity of the Priora into the unprotected world of the market place, they do so in search of 'unas leves mejoras materiales en su forma de vida: nada más' (*16*, p.217). 'Comer y folgar es lo que alegra' (487), declares Nazario, emphasising the beggar's hunger for a taste of freedom in their drab world. But they are only able to define any possible freedom in a material sense, leaving the root of their problem unsolved. Certainly, their sexual frustration, once again a function of their marginal status, is a prime mover in their decision to participate in the scheme, as the outspoken Nazario makes clear when he asserts that 'por las ferias de Francia, hermanos, un espectáculo como el nuestro atraería como moscas a las mujeres' (486). In a world where love is impossible, as it is for the blind beggars, sexuality and its power connotations replace a more meaningful relationship (this is the difficult road that David travels). But when the blind Donato breaks into the snatch of racy song' Cuando Colasa la rodilla enseña' (486) there is more than just a hint of tragic irony here. The use of the verb 'enseñar' suggests that these men, because of their false conciousness, are being driven into the cultivation of what Marcuse called 'false needs',[15] the illusion that freedom can be attained through material satisfaction. But, of course, their material needs are real. Hunger is one of the principal factors which motivate the blind musicians to agree to Valindin's scheme. Once again it is Nazario who muses, 'cierto que llenaríamos la tripa'. Hunger is very much to the fore in *El concierto de San Ovidio*, as Doménech notes (*16*,

---

[14]*To Have or to Be?* (New York: Harper and Row, 1976).
[15]*One-Dimensional Man* (London: Sphere, 1968), p.21.

p.208), both as an image of human lack and dissatisfaction, and as a physical reality particularly widespread in the France of the time. It is hunger in the hospice, where the Priora admits that the soup 'no es abundante' (481), which will drive these men out into the market place.

It is once they move into the economic arena, into the realm of production and profit, that the spectator can begin to identify these blind beggars as exploited in the traditional economic sense. Their stringent circumstances have made them easy prey, as Verdú de Gregorio suggests:

> Los oprimidos no tienen una posición por sí mismos sino que son definidos en la medida de su utilidad para los núcleos superiores. No son libres, en cuanto que sus decisiones están determinadas por una necesidad que les ahoga en la inseguridad y el temor, un pasado angustioso y un futuro sin horizontes. De ahí, la facilidad para ser explotados. *(28,* p.107)

The blind beggars now have something in common with sighted characters like the maid, Catalina, Bernier and even Adriana. They have acquired an exchange value. But in the central tension of their new world, of bourgeois society, they are still the dispossessed, no more free than at the beginning of the play.

This final point is important if we are to understand fully Buero's intentions in choosing this particular moment of history as the framework in which to mount a critique of social and economic oppression. What we have seen so far is that the blind beggars are held in stasis, personal and group, by the dominant power block, the sighted. This is a clear-cut situation which lends itself to several interpretations, as I have suggested. They are the victims of what the South African writer Ronald Segal has called 'the fatal safe denials of the past',[16] a wall of impossibility which results in the type of margination or apartheid to which the beggars are subjected as a group, and the type of fear and despair which corrode the lives of

---

[16]*The Struggle against History* (Harmondsworth: Penguin, 1977), p.132.

Donato and Lucas respectively. In *El concierto de San Ovidio* the 'fatal safe denials of the past' are seen to spring from two general sources whose interrelation can only be understood by careful reference to the period in which the play is set. For in the mid-eighteenth century one of the momentous shifts in human power structures was taking place. It was an age when the hitherto unchallenged superstructure of church and aristocracy had been slowly eroded by the rise of the new monied classes, ushering in the *laissez-faire* spirit of capitalism. The tension between the status quo and nascent commercialism is alluded to adroitly in an early exchange between its two representatives in the play, the Priora and Valindin:

> VALINDIN: ...en Francia nada se logra si no es desde París.
>
> PRIORA: O desde Versalles.
>
> VALINDIN: (Asiente.) O desde Versalles. (477)

This simple exchange reveals, once again, Buero's familiarity with the period in which the play is set. The words refer succinctly to the tension between French political life, still sited in Versalles, and economic life, centralized in Paris and striving to assert its power through the *parlements*. In this way, as the exchange reveals, the 'social and institutional framework of the old regime was a mixture of ancient, medieval and modern', in the words of the historian Olwen Hufton.[17]

There are two reasons why Buero should be so particularly interested in this moment of shifting tensions. Asked why so many writers have turned to the period of the French Revolution, Buero stresses that these writers see there the origins of many of our present socio-political structures:

---

[17]*Europe: Privilege and Protest* (Glasgow: Fontana, 1980), p.299.

> La Revolución francesa fue una de las grandes
> revoluciones de toda la historia humana. Está
> relativamente cerca de nosotros todavía. Es decir, las
> estructuras políticas, sobre todo las políticas, pero
> también en parte sociales, de la sociedad moderna están
> al noventa por ciento basadas aún en el legado de la
> Revolución francesa. Parten de ahí. De modo que todo
> ello evidentemente determina un gran interés de los
> escritores en general por el tema de la Revolución
> francesa, en todos los aspectos, sin olvidar los que tiene
> de terribles y espantosos, claro, pero que parecen ser
> inherentes a una revolución verdadera. (Inter.)

Clearly, Buero does not mean that he views the French Revolution, as does Dickens in *A Tale of Two Cities*, as painful contemporary history. But the central forces which condition Western life today originate in that period. The basic change in the movement from feudal hierarchy to bourgeois capitalism is fundamentally a change in the social identity of man, and is perfectly illustrated in the path that the beggars follow from the Quince Veintes (aristocratic patronage, Church control, charity) to the dangerous forum of the market-place economy (capitalist investment, impresario control, exchange value determined by production). The model that Buero provides of this historical and political change is compelling both in dramatic terms and in terms of the human insights it provides into the nature of life under such a system.

But Buero is doing more than illustrating and clarifying the political and economic forces which condition Western society. *El concierto de San Ovidio*, as a 'parábola', is also concerned to present a radical analysis of Spain at the start of the 1960s, as we saw in Chapter 1. I have already referred to this decade as a troubled one in the course of recent Spanish history. In an attempt to forestall growing national unrest, under increasing pressure from Western liberal democracies, and hoping to hook Spain into the economic miracle now flourishing throughout Europe, the Franco regime began a first and extremely cautious phase of 'apertura', a word to become much more familiar in the 70s. In 1959, as the sociologist Salvador Giner notes,[18] Franco's fascist dictatorship embarked on a new plan of economic expansion packaged and sold to the public as 'desarrollismo'. This entailed the gradual encouragement of an entrepreneurial injection into the economy. Spain's fascist state was slowly evolving into a capitalist economy, no longer rigidly controlled from the centre by the time-hallowed union of powerful families, church and military. This is the second reason why Buero has shown such precision in the delineation of a past moment. It has virtually an exemplary status because of its striking resemblance to the present. In this case, the movement of the blind beggars from paternalistic protection to market-place competition derives from Buero's analysis of the changing economic and social life of the Spanish people.

This, of course, leads us to a re-evaluation of the character of Valindin. He is perhaps one of Buero's finest and most complex portrayals of the unscrupulous man of action (established by now as a favourite character in his theatre), very much more than the conventional one-dimensional villain. These complexities of characterization derive in great part from the complex historical moment which has given birth to the new entrepreneur. Buero is careful to give us enough of Valindin's prehistory to enable us to know that he is not quite the 'self-made man' that Feijoo describes (*20*, p.303). Rather, as Doménech suggests, 'Valindin no es realmente, *todavía*, un hombre en el poder ... sin embargo, sabe cómo puede llegar a serlo' (*16*, p.212). This is an acute observation because it highlights the tension between the ascendant world view of capitalism, soon to become the Western world's driving force, and the feudal system of aristocratic privilege. Valindin himself senses that it is his world view which will subsequently rise through history, as we see in his boast to Adriana that she will see him 'subir como la espuma' (494). His personal rise to wealth which, as he tells the Priora, is his driving ambition (476), is partly a result of business

---

[18]'Spain', in *Contemporary Europe*, ed. Margaret Scotford Archer and Salvador Giner (London: Weidenfield and Nicolson, 1971), pp.125-61, esp. pp.128-29.

acumen (which he clearly has in plenty) and partly a result of his
skill in using patronage. He presents himself at the Quince Veintes
with a letter of recommendation from the Baron de la Tournelle
(476), and later he is very careful to invite his patron to the opening
night of the concert (532). We also learn from Valindin himself that
his patronage (symbolized by the ceremonial sword he is permitted
to carry) derives from his appointment as hairdresser to an unborn
prince, subsequently stillborn (497). The antiquated absurdity of the
situation is not lost either upon Valindin or the play's audience, and
indeed the moment, with Valindin's deliberately ambiguous 'en la
Marina se aprenden muchas cosas' (497), provides one of the very
few moments of light relief in the entire play. But Buero's intention
is nonetheless serious. He is faithfully illustrating the then
widespread practice of the concession of protected sinecures in
which, as Olwen Hufton writes, nothing required the person in
question 'to confine himself to the royal service and stay out of
private business and finance nor suggested that he might not use his
office for his own advantage' (pp.312-13). Thus, in historical terms,
capitalism is beginning to flourish under the umbrella of aristocratic
privilege. The parallel with the Spain of the early 1960s is patent.

It is this gradual and relentless transfer of economic power
which accounts in great part for the Priora's distrust of Valindin
whom she views as a revolutionary threat in a system solidified by
centuries of rule. Her clear dislike for Valindin and her caustic
dismissal of his pretensions to being a gentleman (558) reflect a
classic establishment distaste for the *nouveaux riches*, as well as
reaffirming the play's already clearly defined class axis. Of course,
the very perspicacious Priora is quite right to view Valindin as a
threat, for his way of life with its emphasis on economic liberalism
concedes to ordinary people an importance they could never have
had under the hermetically sealed system of feudal privilege. He will
cater to the tastes of the populace because his profits depend upon
this, and he justifies his choice of profane songs to the Priora by
remarking simply 'son las que el público prefiere' (477). It is a reason
that she probably will find difficult to understand, seeing it as an
unjustifiable piece of egalitarianism. In this way Valindin, as the

symbol of the spirit of capitalist entrepreneurialism, is at this moment a force for positive change, history's first substantial breach in the monolith of the feudal aristocracy. His direct counterpart in Buero's Spain was the 'aperturista', and in Western society he is the figure of the liberal capitalist. In all three of these instances he appears to be breathing the very possibility of freedom into the stultified lives of those who up to this point have consumed their existence in sterile service to a small power elite. It is important to bear this point in mind if we are to understand the strength of David's reaction to Valindin's revolutionary scheme. While the other beggars accept for the sake of '[comidas] algo más sabrosas, sin duda, que nuestra pobre olla' (484), David hails the plan as the means of activating his own dreams of freedom, as we shall see in further detail in Chapter 3. Ironically, therefore, when the Priora leaves it is David who takes up Valindin's cause with his blind companions. Buero himself has referred to this positive aspect of Valindin:

> En aquella época nace el espíritu del capitalismo; pero, en aquella época, el espíritu del capitalismo es un progreso social evidente frente al espíritu feudal y a las monarquías absolutas. Es decir, la independización política del capitalismo, que ya se está independizando socialmente, es un paso adelante evidente en el perfeccionamiento de las sociedades humanas. Luego encontramos, a nuestra vez, en el capitalismo todas las lacras y todos los defectos que lo hacen a veces tan repulsivo. Pero, históricamente, es un paso al frente, no un paso atrás. (Inter.)

Both the Priora's fear and David's excitement generated by Valindin's visit testify to the tremendous force of change that the impresario represents, a sense of dynamism that is communicated to the audience by the stirring allegro from Corelli's Christmas Concerto which fills the slow fade as attention switches from the

Quince Veintes to Valindin's apartments (492).[19] Things, it seems, are on the move.

From this it can be seen that Buero is dramatizing a dialectical sense of history. His phrase 'el perfeccionamiento de las sociedades humanas' reflects a left-wing analysis of the overall movement of history as one system evolves into the next, and as, in this case, feudal hierarchy yields before the driving force of bourgeois capitalism (how David and Valentín Haüy fit into this scheme will be the subject of analysis in Chapter 3). It is this left-wing analysis which leads Buero into an attempt to demythify the liberal capitalist. The theatre audience are able to see that the freedom Valindin will offer the beggars is no more real or substantial than in their restricted existence in the Quince Veintes. The spectators have shared in David's excitement through the medium of the allegro, but this tangible sense of anticipation is dashed almost immediately. In broad terms, as the true nature of Valindin's character emerges in the next scene, and the extent of his deceit becomes manifest, the audience realize that there is little for the blind beggars to look forward to here. They will still be a service class, in political terms, and dominated objects, in existential terms, The alienation remains the same. The warning that Buero is sounding through Valindin to the Spanish society of the 1960s is clear. In *El concierto de San Ovidio* the dramatist is cautioning his countrymen, as he did also in *Un soñador para un pueblo*, that they must not betray their interests, that they must ensure a constantly critical attitude to the changes which take place in national life. Verdú stresses that Valindin's concept of man is just as contemptuous of human potential for

---

[19]Arcangelo Corelli (1653-1713) has an important thematic link with the play, in addition to the use that Buero makes of his music in heightening the emotional impact of certain scenes. As an early pioneer in the development and acceptance of the *concerto grosso*, the forerunner of the classical concerto form, Corelli stands as another figure who has contributed to the breaking of new ground in history. Moreover, it is quite possible that Buero chose a *concerto grosso* because its form, in which the soloist competes openly with the other players in a developing musical dialogue, is reminiscent in a very broad sense of the respective battles undertaken by David and Haüy. See Nicholas (*24*, p.70) and Dixon (*15*, pp.34-35).

development as that of the Priora. He refers to a famous quotation from Lampedusa's *Il gattopardo*:

> El contenido de la respuesta de Valindin es el moderno equivalente de la frase que Lampedusa pone en boca de uno de sus personajes: 'Si queremos que todo siga como está, s preciso que todo cambie.' (*28*, p.109)

In basic terms, while the material conditions of life may change, human beings remain imprisoned in a reified universe, objects among objects, unable to exercise the freedom they crave. *El concierto de San Ovidio*, like *Il gattopardo*, shows that while the superstructure of power may change, society requires a much more radical transformation if the blind beggars of this world are ever to free themselves from their 'constante marginación' (*28*, p.113). (Buero's view as to how this transformation may be achieved is illustrated through the characters of Haüy and David, as we shall see in Chapter 3.)

The writer's radical analysis of the features of the capitalist ethic results in the depiction of a grasping and ruthless impresario. Buero stresses that the character of Valindin is conceived with a large measure of ideological hindsight. Following on from his statement that in its moment the capitalist ethic was a liberating impulse, he notes:

> Claro, aunque yo acabo de hacer una especie de canto histórico al capitalismo en sus inicios o en su independización política, evidentemente Valindin es un personaje muy negative. Es un sinvergüenza, sencillamente. Entonces, claro, este hombre ya está visto por una óptica posterior, con una óptica marxista. Pero el que yo le trate tan fríamente en mi obra no significa que, porro contraste, esté haciendo el canto de Luis XV, ni mucho menos ...(Inter.)

While the audience may be in some doubt in the first scene as to whether or not Valindin's intentions are strictly honourable, his subsequent conversation with Adriana, as we have mentioned, will rapidly rid them of any illusion. His motto of 'tiempo de hambre, tiempo de negocios' (496) reveals a philosophy that is totally exploitative, unresponsive in the extreme to genuine needs. This is precisely the type of relationship he will strike up with the blind beggars, and we witness an immediate foretaste of this in his first exchanges with Adriana. As Jordan has implied, the patriarchal domination that Valindin exercises over his mistress anticipates his control over the beggars (*23*, p.433). Valindin's relationship with Adriana is underwritten by economic power. He boasts to her:

> ¡Pero entraste a trabajar con Valindin y Valindin pudo contigo! (Ríe.) Me costó lo mío, lo admito. ¿Cuántas espantadas me diste? (495)

Buero points to one significant detail which tells of the poverty of Adriana's background when he notes that 'su físico denuncia a la campesina vigorosa, a quien la ciudad no logró afinar del todo' (494). She is part of that great wave of the hungry who came flooding into Paris after the failure of crop after crop. This is her fundamental link with Bernier and the beggars, and in particular with Donato and David, both of whom we are told come from a rural background. In this way, she is very much a victim of the hardnosed philosophy of 'tiempo de hambre, tiempo de negocios', as she herself insinuates when she replies to Valindin 'Y de mujeres' (496). She is no less an object in Valindin's world than the blind beggars, no freer than a pet animal, as her petname of 'galga' suggests (495).[20] Buero points out at a later stage that this paternalism is underpinned by a willingness to resort to violence in order to maintain power when Valindin threatens to tie her up in order to prevent her from leaving him (583). The dangerous inequalities inherent in this type of relationship suddenly become manifest as Adriana's petname

---

[20]The legend 'A la levrette' appears over the stage in the engraving which inspired the play. See 2, pp.92-93.

translates itself into brutal reality. But normally, as is the case with the blind beggars as well, they are masked by simple materialistic bribes. Valindin presents Adriana with a golden necklace 'en señal de la alegría por la firma del contrato' (495), and David, also aware of the nature of Valindin's hold on her, taunts her bitterly with '¿Qué vas a sacar tú de esto? ¿Un vestido a la góndola? ¿Tal vez una joya?' (518).

It is by deceit that Valindin survives and subsequently grows in strength. Underlying the momentum of his material bribes is the momentum of a moral deceit. His initial deception of the Priora, to which she is a more or less willing party, is rapidly followed by the demonstration of his ability to disguise his unequal relationship with Adriana with the language of conventional flattery - 'mi galga se ha puesto guapa ... ¡Si hasta parece una dama de la corte!' (494). It is Valindin's plausible fluency which is most evident in his first meeting with the Priora. His moral deceit is particularly reflected in his dishonest appropriation of the philosophy of the day as a cloak for his ambition. Sensing a change in the times, a surging popular desire for freedom, Valindin latches onto the new philanthropy to justify his actions morally. He presents himself to both beggars and Bernier as a benefactor (507), and he adopts a heavily paternalistic style of language, designed to convince his underlings of the happiness and security he affords them and to foster in them certain filial responses: 'Os he llamado [hijos míos] porque me habéis demostrado que se puede confiar en vuestro celo' (568). Again, the parallel with the Spanish society of 1962 is evident. The freedom that Valindin espouses is the freedom to exploit. It is neither the philosophical freedom of Voltaire or the political liberty of Jean-Jacques Rousseau, as he is careful to assure the Priora (478). It is an empty rhetoric which ably takes the measure of each situation in order to further its interests. Thus, Valindin does not hesitate to tell the Priora that his scheme 'posee su cara espiritual' (478) in order to salve her conscience whilst, at the same time, showing a willingness to engage in hardline negotiations with her (479). This encapsulates well the moral deceit which informs the material bribes. It is the offering of a freedom above and beyond material advancement. Here

Buero is clearly informing the Spanish people that they are faced
with a new system whose central concept of man is no more
liberating than the old, although it inspires support through its loose
association with, and able exploitation of, 'las nuevas ideas' (478).
Once again, Ronald Segal's views are applicable to *El concierto de
San Ovidio*:

> The system does not, and cannot, satisfy the moral
> desires that it excites. It does not, and cannot, provide
> the personal freedom, and the equality of opportunity,
> the compassion and security, the experience of extended
> individuality that it claims. (p.47)

This, of course, explains the weight of David's subsequent
disillusion, as we shall see in Chapter 3. He is fooled initially by an
entrepreneur who skilfully conceals his ruthless economic
pragmatism under the cloak of humanitarian concern. The tension
between reality and appearances is discernible from the start with the
knowing double meaning that he concedes to the word 'beneficioso'
as he speaks to the Priora (476). The smiling face of capitalism that
Buero paints through Valindin - 'sé unir lo útil a lo bueno' (496) - is
taken almost to the length of caricature. The scene in which Valindin
coaxes a bemused and reluctant Bernier to acknowledge the force for
good which he, Valindin, represents in his impoverished existence is
a case in point. We must also bear in mind that the tears which
spring regularly to Valindin's eyes are, as Feijoo points out, very
much part of a burgeoning romanticized sensibility which the
impresario ably exploits (*20*, p.302). His driving goal is profit, and
both ideas and people are legitimate means for furthering this end.

Clearly transparent remarks like 'peco de sensible' (478) and
'me conmueve tanto', as he considers the spiritual blessings he will
secure in the wake of his 'ofrenda' to the hospice (558), lend
dramatic appeal to the overall characterization of Valindin.
Moreover, he is plainly a man who has a gnawing hollow at the
centre of his being (this is a problem common to all those in Buero's
theatre who, like the torturers in *La doble historia del doctor Valmy*,

sacrifice their basic humanity to inhuman goals). Apart from his death, Valindin is symbolically punished by Buero two ways. Firstly, he suffers from an irredeemable loneliness (the consequence of his lack of human solidarity), which he assuages in solitary 'juergas' (494) and a fondness for alcohol. Secondly, although his final despairing cry of ¡Adriana!' (592) suggests that his love for her was surprisingly real, as David himself believes (596), he is unable to inspire any response in her. It is a love destroyed by the system of values that his own ethos has created. And the children he longs for are denied to him by his mistress who can feel no passion for him and who must suspect that, if she has been a simple extension of his property, then any future offspring could only represent a posthumous continuation of that same property. As Chapter 3 will show, both Adriana's love and her promise of children are symbolically given to David.

All of this helps to humanize the figure of Valindin. But, as a man, he still comes across to the audience as distasteful in the extreme. This is, of course, as Buero intends it to be. It is primarily the tremendous disjunction between his words and his actions which distances the audience emotionally from Valindin. Moreover, Valindin's readiness to resort to violence if his plausible rhetoric fails is an important factor in the spectators' assessment of his character. There are two lingering background presences in *El concierto de San Ovidio*, the pervasive air of fear and hunger, and the constant threat of violence designed to keep the consequent human revolt in check. Valindin both forms part of and benefits from this second presence. The irrationality of his outbursts to Adriana and the beggars, his constant fluctuation between the promise of reward and the threat of punishment, his intimidation of Donato and his physical brutality with David, all serve to define Valindin as a ruthless man of action. The 'escribano' (493), the policemen, the sinister 'lettres de cachet', the threat of torture and the eventual execution all combine to form an image of a society clearly founded upon legally sanctioned violence. Valindin is an integral part of this world.

Through Valindin, therefore, Buero undertakes a fundamental process of demythification of the new society emerging from the old. The impresario represents the glittering prizes of gain and freedom, ultimately illusory, dangled before those who are prepared to move from protectionism into the exploitative and acquisitive world of the market place. Despite its pretensions to a dynamic way of life, this new system is as static as the one which preceded it. But, of course, that this new way of life should appear so attractive is a direct consequence of the hierarchical world which has gone before. It is in this light that we should consider the Priora. She stands in direct opposition to Valindin, the intrepid entrepreneur whose sole concern is material gain, insisting on the values of passive interiority. Whereas Valindin is constantly aware of time, checking his watch, rushing to meet deadlines, very much the 'hombre emprendedor y eficaz' (476), the world of the Priora and the Quince Veintes appears timeless. The Latin psalms and prayers with which the play opens, and which Valindin significantly interrupts (475), and the gloomy interior of the hospice serve to convey dramatically to the audience the immobility of her world. The 'in saecula saeculorum' and the call to the beggars for 'un Ave María por nuestro muy amado rey y protector Luis XV y por todos los príncipes y princesas de su sangre' (475) parallels the union of Church and State in the Franco regime and the timeless conception of Spanishness on which it was based. Moreover, it is a call to prayer which would remind many members of a Spanish audience of their own prayers in school for Franco, the *pater patriae*.

It would perhaps be unjust to accuse Buero of unequivocally pinning the representative of Christianity to the wall. His attack is not directed personally against the Priora. Indeed, as is the case with her counterpart in *Un soñador para un pueblo*, Villasanta, she is endowed with certain redeeming traits - her perspicacity and acerbic wit which permit her to deal with and see through Valindin. Once again, this is wholly in keeping with Buero's methods of characterization, by which no character is presented as the one-dimensional incarnation of an idea or moral maxim. The result is, of course, the creation of characters whose emotional shifts and moral complexity will keep an audience's attention. But, for the purposes of criticism, it is misleading to begin to isolate characters from the dramatic structures which embody them, and it is in the context of her principal interaction, with the beggars, that we must look at the Priora. In this way we can see clearly that Buero's attack is directed against those social norms created by the Church's political dominance, and is not a critique of Christian values *per se*. This impression is confirmed by Buero's assertion in an interview that 'la Iglesia, desde el punto de vista de la acción social, ha tenido a lo largo de la Historia en general una actuación funesta, no encuentro otra palabra' (*13*, p.48). This opinion is broadened into a more specific analysis of cause and effect which throws direct light onto Buero's whole conception of the Quince Veintes. The point that he makes is a rejection, rooted in left-wing ideology, of institutionalized and individual charity:

> Este hincapié en dar limosna, en la caridad, la Iglesia no
> lo ignoraba, era justo la manera de que nunca se
> resolvieran las cosas, de que el 'status' injusto siga así y
> que cada cual se salve practicando la caridad. (*13*, p.48)

The basic point is that charity deals solely with the symptoms and not with the root causes of a problem, and that too many people salve their conscience by a simple act of charity rather than turning their attention to the deeper issues. This explains the ambivalence in the characterization of the Priora. Her compassionate concern for the blind humanizes her, especially when we contrast her attitudes with those of Valindin. But unlike the active compassion of Valentín Haüy, hers is a form of pity which wounds because it is based on a sense of the irredeemable misery of its object. The beggars accept her charity, as they must, but their resentment burns through at times (485-86).

It is perhaps opportune to remind ourselves at this point that the religious control of the Quince Veintes is entirely Buero's own invention. Here we have one of the creative touches which turn history into parable, which elucidate more clearly the exemplary meaning of the past. Any attempt to present an analysis of the strands of influence in the slowly evolving political and economic landscape of Francoist Spain would be meaningless without reference to the Church, and in particular to its role as a conservative agent. Accordingly, the primary aspect of the Priora's interaction with the beggars that Buero highlights is the negative impact of her teaching on their lives. An obvious hesitancy informs her conflicting advice to the beggars. On one hand is her belief that 'cuando se nos ofrece algo en bien de estos desheredados estamos obligados a poner la mano...' (478), a coy reference to conscience which Valindin, probably quite correctly, interprets as an indirect allusion to money, and on the other is her conviction that an orchestra composed of blind musicians is an impossible and unworthy dream. In this way she constantly minimizes the beggars' self-belief, instilling in them the same hopeless conviction that change is an impossibility.

Implicit in the Priora's view of these men is the abstract concept of original sin as a moral sign of man's social untrustworthiness and inability to transform the kingdom of this world. The blindness of the beggars is seen as an indication from God that their lives are to be wholly devoted to prayer:

> Dios no consiente la ceguera de estos trescientos desdichados para perder sus almas, sino para que ofrezcan oraciones por las calles, lo mismo que en los velatorios y las iglesias ... Ellos han nacido para rezar mañana y tarde, pues es lo único que, en su desgracia, podrán hacer siempre bien. (477)

Her words, reinforced by the total conviction of the final future tense and 'siempre', condemn the future of these men to the mediocrity of their continuing past. The Priora is perpetuating a system whose impact on the personality is wholly destructive and whose stress on the beggars' paramount function as one of hopeless devotion leaves no time or stimulus for independent action or thought. Her attitude is a simple version of that same political paternalism which Buero attacked so convincingly in *Un soñador para un pueblo*, principally through Ensenada's cynical '¿qué se puede hacer con un pueblo así?' (214). Buero is really broaching two specific factors of Spanish life here. Firstly, he is trying to cope with and expose the limitations of that sense of national pessimism which has been the bitter fruit of Spain's rapid historical decline and eclipse. More specifically, he is communicating a valid image of the patronizing system of government which since 1939 had declared the Spanish people morally unfit to control their own political destiny. In both cases, he is criticizing any system which encourages or forces the individual to retreat into a wholly private or contemplative existence at the expense of involvement in the external world. For Buero, as *El concierto de San Ovidio* reveals, there can be no natural authority or hierarchy, religious or political, which can justifiably require this withdrawal into passivity.

The blatant contempt for human possibilities which typifies the views of both the Priora and Valindin springs, in the former case, from the historicist belief that history is the inevitable unfolding of God's plan,[21] and in the latter from the cynical conviction that material gain will automatically exclude man's individual sense of purpose, that everyone has their price. The result in both cases is submission and alienation. But *El concierto de San Ovidio*, as a parable, is concerned to show how the mould of submission may be broken and the alienation overcome. This is the struggle undertaken by David and Haüy, the struggle against history itself.

---

[21]Historicism, in this sense, refers to the notion that history is created by forces beyond the control of man. For the most devastating criticism of this view, see Karl Popper's *The Poverty of Historicism* (London: Routledge and Kegan Paul, 1957).

3 *The Historical Hero*

As we turn our attention to the characters of David and Valentín Haüy, it may perhaps be opportune to remind ourselves of the dialectical tension that exists at the heart of Buero's theatre, and which is reflected as we have seen, in the 'moriremos caminando' of *Llegada de los dioses*. On one hand is the author's consciousness of human reification and historical stagnation, embodied in the blind beggars, and on the other is his belief that these are circumstantial conditions against which man can meaningfully struggle. This conviction is in part ideologically motivated, reflecting the Marxist idea that the individual defines his life through action rather than passivity or withdrawal. But the pressure of Buero's own humanity also leads him to the awareness, that we find no less in writers as different as Unamuno and Eugene O'Neill, that man derives vitality from the very act of struggle itself. The tragic dimension that this introduces into *El concierto de San Ovidio* will be the subject of analysis in Chapter 4 but it should be stressed here that Buero views struggle as both a personal need and a political phenomenon. In this way, perhaps rather like Bertolt Brecht, Buero Vallejo becomes a kind of theoretician of struggle. Whilst recognizing that the will and need to struggle are an inevitable and necessary part of individual vitality, Buero goes beyond Unamuno's depiction of man living and feeding off the act of struggle itself, by pointing to the historical and collective implications of man's need to assert himself in the face of hostile circumstances. Struggle, for Buero, is not simply an end in itself. It is movement towards a defined historical goal, the nature of which should be clear from the discussion in Chapter 1. It is the humanistic drive to establish man himself as the supreme value of all our social and economic structures. In *El concierto de San Ovidio* both David and Haüy illustrate the personal and political dimensions implicit in the individual act of revolt, and it would be a mistake to attempt to separate these two aspects. David's personal struggle is made significant by the whole process of progressive change that it anticipates, and which is initiated by Haüy. These personal terms in which David's struggle is cast are, of course, perfectly valid ones, and the dramatist never seeks to ignore that the demands of our intimate, private world are frequently more pressing than those of the wider political realm. But, as this chapter will show, the two are in reality inextricably bound together, and the fundamental aim of *El concierto de San Ovidio* is, in this respect, a concern, akin to that of any leftist ideology, to rescue the individual from the 'insignificance of finitude'[22] by revealing how he or she may contribute to genuine historical achievement.

Accordingly, the play has what we might call a broadly dualistic attitude towards truth. In one way it sets about the demythification of the fictions which cocoon man's life in an acquisitive and entrepreneurial society. Running parallel to this is the creation of an authentic and meaningful myth of change, a psychological truth conceived as a rallying call for a people sunk in a deep-rooted sense of impossibility. Buero has stressed the dual function of art, emphasizing that while the exploding of myth and false assumptions in the name of truth is relatively easy, the real validity of any art form lies in its construction of new possibilities, of images of increasingly relevant ways of focusing faith:

> Ante la insistencia ya casi rutinaria, con que se viene invocando la actitud desmitificadora como la única plausible en un teatro que se pretende acorde con la realidad del mundo de hoy, suelo reiterar, desde hace tiempo, el papel positivo de lo mítico. Desmitificar es saludable y necesario, pero no es, creo, la fórmula definitiva de un arte finalmente desenajenado. Desmitificar es relativamente fácil; la dificultad - y el hallazgo - del arte consiste en volver a mitificar, de

---

[22]Alasdair MacIntyre, *Marxism and Christianity* (London: Duckworth, 1983), p.112.

> modo más real, con los escombros de las
> mitificaciones.(*10*, p.73)

It is not difficult to see how *El concierto de San Ovidio* fits in with
this. On one level, as Chapter 2 showed, the play offers a
convincingly realistic analysis of contemporary man's predicament
in a hostile and dishonest system, projected backwards in time but
nonetheless valid for that. This is coupled with an essentially poetic
affirmation of hope in the possibility of progress and change - the
human face of struggle, so to speak. This is the new myth of the
theatre of Buero Vallejo, an image of hope which gives rise to the
type of character we may call the historical hero, the individual who
carries the pressing weight of Buero's historical faith upon his
shoulders.

The term 'hero' is clearly one which bristles with potential
misinterpretation. In an aggressively egalitarian age like ours it
appears to smack heavily of Nietzsche's superman or Thomas
Carlyle's apotheosis of the 'great man'. Indeed, there may well be
some measure of common ground between Buero's presentation of
his historical hero and the German philosopher's depiction of the
new saviour of an abject and spineless mankind. At the heart of the
Spanish dramatist's thought lies a compelling tension between a
Marxist statement of belief in the ultimate ability of the collectivity
to develop and grow towards the fulfilment of its political destiny,
and a markedly Nietzschean tendency to show how the collective
will has become so successfully neutralized that one man must take
upon himself, willingly or not, the role of motor force. In his essay
'Masters of the Modern Theatre' Robert Corrigan underlines the
importance of the hero figure in post-modernist drama:

> One of the most important functions of the hero, both in
> art and life, is to supply those images, values and ethical
> standards which people aspire to and which they would
> like to incorporate into their own lives. It would seem,
> however, that increasingly our modern industrialized
> society not only does not need heroes, but also actually
> suppresses or perverts our need of them ... Only the

system, then, is important, and it fills men's remaining need for heroes by promoting celebrities, those heroes of the surface who play their constantly shifting roles well.[23]

The history plays of Buero Vallejo, in particular *Un soñador para un pueblo* and *El concierto de San Ovidio*, are concerned to reassert the role of the hero, in the words of Buero 'uno de los motores que elevan a la especie humana como conjunto, y le abren puertas' (Inter.). The Marxist/Nietzschean framework into which Buero slots his hero figure accounts for the apparent political contradictions in the plays of the historical cycle. In the case of *Un soñador para un pueblo*, in particular, contemporary reviewers were offended by what they felt to be the ideological unsoundness of the work, complaining that the people, the highest unit of value in the Marxist scheme of things, are portrayed as being blind to their own interests and as requiring the paternalistic intervention of the individual dreamer of the title. This is very much the final situation of *El concierto de San Ovidio* as well, as Jordan has also complained (23, p.448). But Buero defended his ideological stance in *Un soñador para un pueblo* by declaring that in this keywork of the historical cycle he raises the 'pueblo' 'casi a una categoría ontológica', meaning by this that the play reveals that popular liberation and the ultimate purpose of history are one and the same. This ontological dimension, the vision of a new future, is made explicit at two climactic moments in *El concierto de San Ovidio*. A future of clear-sighted justice and freedom is symbolically promised to David when Adriana declares that 'nuestros hijos verán' (599), and Valentín Haüy tells the audience that his reforming work is achieving that goal in the person of his blind students when he foresees that 'lo lograrán... algún día' (604). In this sense, David and Haüy, the clear historical heroes of the work, are linked by a consciousness which is oriented towards the creation of new and better conditions for their fellows.

---

[23]'Masters of the Modern Theatre', in *Masterpieces of the Modern Spanish Theatre* (New York: Collier, 1967), p.21.

The hero in the theatre of Buero Vallejo is, therefore, the embodiment of a speculative hope, the transmission of an image of the struggle for change to an audience chained, as we have seen, to an abiding and destructive sense of stagnation and impotence. Accordingly, as has already been noted, Buero's characterization of the beggars especially derives from a sadly realistic assessment of Western man's surrender to the one-dimensional existence imposed upon him. The playwright's respect for reality and his hatred of mystification prevent him from romanticizing the political awareness of the people or of over-estimating the executive capacity of marginal groups. Instead, perhaps with a greater degree of humanity, Buero seeks to show that the limited consciousness of those groups of characters who represent the collectivity in his plays is a direct function of their tremendously limited social being. In the specific case of the blind beggars of *El concierto de San Ovidio* we see a clear demonstration of Feurbach's materialist deflation of idealism: 'If because of hunger, of misery, you have no foodstuff in your body, you likewise have no stuff for morality in your head.'[24] The danger, of course, as Buero tries to show in the play, is that the struggle for life, the sheer battle for survival, will come to replace altogether man's determination to construct a better world. Buero's awareness of the ideological importance of the people, reflected in the phrase 'una categoría ontológica', brings him to symbolize their unchained potential in and through the figure of the hero. In this respect he runs counter to Brecht's celebrated and ideologically rooted dismissal of the hero. The words 'unhappy the land that needs a hero', in the words echo still round our theatres. But Buero might well answer in the words of the Argentine director Augusto Boal who, aware that his nation no less than Spain has been subjected to a systematic campaign of official distortion and misinformation, can state simply, 'but we are not a happy land'.[25] For both Boal and Buero ideological purity must be tempered by a respect for reality.

Thus, the tension between David and the other beggars enables Buero to use *El concierto de San Ovidio* as an extended exploration

[24]MacIntyre, *Marxism and Christianity*, pp.11-29, esp. pp.24-28.
[25]*Theatre of the Oppressed* (London: Pluto, 1979), p.150.

of man as the object of social and historical forces, and man as the conscious subject struggling for liberation. It is simultaneously man's tragedy and his strength that he must struggle for his political and existential independence. Here Buero clearly rejects what he obviously feels to be Brechtian idealism:

> Lo ideal es que un pueblo no necesite héroes para marchar adelante y mejorarse. Aunque dicho sea de paso, más bien parece, a pesar de haberlo dicho Brecht, una consigna más reformista que revolucionaria. Un pueblo sin héroes, al estilo suizo o sueco, que va progresivamente mejorando sin necesidad de héroes, es más bien reformista que revolucionario, porque la revolución en la cual creía Brecht inevitablemente necesita héroes. Pero también estoy por decir que la vida diaria, aunque no sea de una etapa revolucionaria, también los necesita. Es decir, el heroísmo marca uno de los buenos techos del ser humano.(Inter.)

Two points are of immediate interest here. Firstly, Buero clearly considers the figure of the hero to be an integral element in the creation of a revolutionary consciousness. In other words, the hero in Buero's theatre is geared to stimulate the historical imagination of the audience. In this respect, as we have seen, the hero primarily provides an image of potentiality actualized through struggle. But Buero also makes it clear that the hero, if he is to prove palatable to a contemporary audience, must bear no elitist stamp. And here Buero parts company most decisively from Nietszche. As *El concierto de San Ovidio* shows, the hero is the ordinary man who undertakes the creative struggle against circumstances, who asserts himself in the face of injustice and who, in doing so, in the words of Buero, opens the doors of possibility to his companions. The fundamental link between David and Haüy is that both speak alternatives (or literally cry them out) and fight for the potentialities of others beyond the self.

For the hero to work on this level the character must be more than the incarnation of an ideological stance or of a moral maxim. He or she must also embody a whole and, to the audience at least, satisfying series of individual fears and aspirations. It is significant that the dramatist provides a certain amount of prehistory for both David and Haüy. In a scene late in the final act, when David has overcome his radical distrust of Adriana, he confides the details of his background to her. Reading between the lines, and in spite of David's rather curious failure to put two and two together, we can see that the boy was in all probability the unacknowledged product of an illicit union between master and servant (598). This fact, coupled to the incident in which the young boy is blinded by fireworks during a party in the castle, makes of David a victim of the privileged in every sense of the word. Haüy's prehistory is not so traumatic. But in the second act, when he is ejected from the café by Latouche and his henchmen, his social impotence and lack of any influence are quite clear. The thematic implications of both characters' ability to proceed and struggle heroically despite their lowly background are drawn out explicitly by Haüy in one of the key passages of the work:

> Yo era un desconocido sin relieve: Valentín Haüy, intérprete de lenguas y amante de la música. Nadie. Pero el hombre más oscuro puede mover montañas si lo quiere. (604)

This expresses the crux of the matter. The most apparently insignificant of people can struggle against seemingly insuperable odds. This is the conviction that underpins the characterization of David and Haüy alike. The former's struggle is primarily a revolutionary refusal to succumb to the overpowering factors of poverty and blindness which have enchained his class. He revolts against the defining circumstances of his life, as Doménech notes when he writes that 'ceguera y pobreza constituyen las dos caras - inseparables - de la realidad del personaje' (16, p.215). Similarly, Haüy's struggle is that of the reformer whose basic battle is waged with the spiritual poverty and blindness which defined his peergroup. I shall return to the relationship between revolution and reform at a later point in this chapter, but for the moment it is enough to bear in mind that through David and Haüy the dramatist seeks to provide an image of achievement, personal and collective, which rescues the individual from the meaningless sojourn of existence in the Hospice (David)[26] or from the idle, frittering waste of the bourgeoisie (Haüy). Let us see what forms their achievement takes.

It is David who carries the weight of the audience's attention and sympathy through the play. He is the most complex character in the work, both in terms of his own motivation and of the various levels of interaction he has with other characters. And it is also David who is responsible for introducing the principal elements of conflict into the play, primarily with Valindin, but also with the other blind beggars, notably Donato, and Adriana. Both on and off stage, the character rapidly establishes himself as the pivotal point of the work, around which all dramatic conflict revolves. This poses an interesting problem of dramatization for Buero in the first scenes of the play. It is important that David is somehow differentiated from the other beggars without destroying at too early a point their sense of being a group, thereby dissipating the aura of collective misery and hopelessness that emanates from them. This is achieved by highlighting almost immediately two of the main facets of David's personality. He is identified virtually from the start as a dreamer. He has collected less the other beggars because 'se me páso el tiempo' (482), the first hint in the play that David will be, at least in the first instance, the contemplative who stands in opposition, as always in Buero's theatre, to the ruthless and grasping man of action. Secondly, he is also identified as a man of caution. A good actor would communicate David's rising excitement (perhaps rather understated in the stage direction 'nervioso', 484) as the Priora

---

[26]Antonio Machado's 'El Hospicio' (poem 100 of *Campos de Castilla*) centres on a similarly double-edged metaphor, the 'hospicio' as a symptom of a country deep in stagnation, and the symbol of mankind, lost in despair, aimlessly awaiting death.

outlines Valindin's scheme to the incredulous beggars. But David
will not be drawn into premature comment, preferring to withold his
opinion until the rest have expressed theirs.

It is only when the beggars have echoed the Priora's sense of
impossibility that David eventually erupts. Meanwhile he has
distanced himself both physically and emotionally from the beggars'
discussion of the relative material benefits that may accrue from
their participation in the scheme. In fact, this distancing deliberately
highlights, as do several similar incidents in the play, the beggars'
vulnerability to the simplest of physical circumstances when Nazario
asks anxiously, '¿Eh, David? (Silencio.) ¿Se ha ido?' (488). David's
first major speech of the play stresses the importance of a positive
approach:

> ¡Habéis creído decir sí, pero habéis dicho no! ¡Aceptáis
> por la comida, por las mozas! ¡Pero si pensáis en
> vuestros violines os come el pánico. ¡Tenéis que decir sí
> a vuestros violines! (Va de uno a otro, exaltado.) Ese
> hombre no es un iluso; sabe lo que quiere. Adivino que
> haremos buenas migas. El ha pensado lo que yo pensaba,
> lo que llevaba años madurando sin atreverme a decirlo.
> (488-89)

These words reveal David as above all else a character in personal
revolt against circumstances which threaten to reduce his life to a
meaningless stasis. His description of a plan upon which he has
brooded for years 'sin atreverme a decirlo' not only explains David's
subsequent hostility towards and distrust of sighted characters like
Adriana, but also reveals an imaginative capacity hidebound by
circumstances as yet insurmountable. The symbol of the violin
assumes its full complexity here. It is initially a sign of private
consolation - we know that David's first violin was given to him as a
compensation for the incident in which he was blinded (598), and,
secondly, throughout the play he withdraws into the solitary playing
of the adagio from Corelli's Christmas Concerto (see note 19, above)
at moments when the intensity of his imaginative world makes

reality unbearable (this is linked to his obsession with Melania de Salignac, as we shall see later). But with his encouragement to his companions to 'decir sí a vuestros violines' David foresees the possibility of converting the violin into an active instrument of liberation. Jordan expresses this well:

> [David's] own project - the bid for an authentic relationship between player and instrument in a genuine orchestra - still inhabits the discourse of the unspeakable, i.e. that of madness, which, in terms of the dominant definitions of 'truth', literally goes unheard. (*23*, p.439)

The violin, therefore, becomes a potent symbol of a sociopolitical struggle undertaken through the medium of culture. On the most obvious level, this is a fine metaphor for the resistance of the committed writer working under Franco. In another way, it reveals an awareness on the part of the dramatist that any insulation of culture from politics is a central factor in the rise of the economic imperialism so fervently championed by Valindin. In this way, *El concierto de San Ovidio* addresses what Buero clearly sees as the crisis in contemporary culture by showing that culture is a potentially liberating force when it moves out from the realm of aesthetic subjectivity into an engagement with the external world.

As Jordan's words imply, we meet David at a crucial point of his development, concretely at the moment in which the will to succeed, previously swamped under a destructive sense of impossibility, moves from the world of imaginative aspiration into that of practical reality. Through the figure of Valindin, David glimpses the chance of a human reply to the dead hand of traditional belief which has kept both him and his fellows immersed in stagnation. In the words of Ronald Segal, he himself will become the 'reply to the fatal safe denials of the past'. It is this apparent sudden accreditation of a private world of dream which explains David's immediate identification with Valindin, and which accounts for the subsequent strength of his disillusion. His 'adivino que haremos

buenas migas' parallels the hopeful reaction of many Spaniards in
1962 to the 'aperturistas'. The yearning for a new and more
comfortable future finds an apparent response in the promise of the
development of an enticing consumer society. Just as David foresees
the possibility of breaking the divisive moulds of blind/sighted, as
Verdú notes (*28*, p.115), so radical and disaffected sectors of
Spanish society sensed that the closed door of the regime may be
slowly opening to them. Both character and people, like James
Joyce's Stephen Dedalus, oppressed by the narrowness of Irish
politics and tradition, feel themselves to be 'awakening from the
nightmare of history'.[27] But unlike Joyce's hero, whose retreat from
history leads him to embrace an extreme subjectivity, David
spearheads the legitimate attempt to redefine history, to open up its
processes to the dispossessed and the disaffected. In this way,
through the exemplary story of David, *El concierto de San Ovidio*
warns not just the 'vencidos' of Spanish society, but all those in
pursuit of greater equality and freedom, of the dangers of rushing
into unholy alliances. The bitterness with which David assails
Valindin at the end of the play is sharpened by shattered illusion:

> Cuando la priora nos habló de vos dije: '¡Al fin! Yo
> ayudaré a ese hombre y lo veneraré toda mi vida'.
> Después... comprendí que se trataba de hacer reír. (589)

The encoded meaning for a nation which senses itself to be on the
threshold of a new era is quite clear.

With the benefit of hindsight we find it ironical that it is the
blind David's sixth sense of a new freedom beyond the imagination
of the others that blinds him, in the first instance at least, to the real

nature of Valindin's scheme. But his mistake is one of a quixotic
generosity. Buero may very well be reminding his audience of the
need for clear-sighted analysis of new proposals and developments,
and we may expect to find a recommendation of this nature in a
radical writer, but he is no less concerned to show that progress in
individual and collective affairs is not the fruit of reason alone.

---

[27]*Ulysses* (London: Granada, 1977), p.471.

Indeed, we can appreciate how in David's situation imagination can be the sole antidote to the reactionary logic of the Priora's system. This notion allows the dramatist to expand the meanings of the play's dominant metaphor, that of blindness. In one way, David is blind to much in life, as all human beings are, our vision foreshortened by the determinant factors of our social being and of the human condition itself. Moreover, specific aspects of the play serve to highlight David's metaphorical blindness. We have already looked at his initially uncritical acceptance of Valindin. But he is also slow to recognize Adriana as a natural ally. The spectator can see clearly that David's hostility towards her is in part a result of his growing disillusion with Valindin's plan. But it is also apparent that it springs from the sexual tension between the sighted woman and the blind men, a tension that Valindin himself suggests to Adriana that she should exploit in order to further his scheme. This tension between Adriana and David is made explicit at one point in the First Act:

> ADRIANA: ... ¿Qué sabéis vos de mujeres de carne y hueso?
>
> DAVID: Frío.) Sé a lo que saben y sé que saben bien. No les pido más.
>
> ADRIANA: (Vibrante.) Las pagas y te vas, ¿eh? ¡Un cerdo como todos!
>
> DAVID: ¡Eso tú lo sabrás!
>
> ADRIANA: ¡Sí que lo sé! ¡Los hombres pagáis porque no os atrevéis a pedir más! (518-19)

Adriana makes the general and the particular point succinctly. Enclosed for so many years in the hermetically sealed world of the blind, David has been unable to find any degree of love or solidarity, the political counterpart of love, in his life, other than the paternal relationship he has established with Donato, the youngest of the beggars. In common with the other blind beggars, as I mentioned in

Chapter 2, David is locked into relationships with women that can never rise above the solely sexual.

But David's blindness is also the sign of an initiation into a form of knowledge based not upon the rational analysis of what is already existent, but which instead derives from the imaginative re-creation of that which should be. This figure of the blind visionary who exposes the limitations of reason is, of course, not a new one in the literature of the Western tradition. And in keeping with this tradition, David moves in the course of the play from the consciousness of blindness as an impediment to the certain knowledge and incisive perceptions he reveals in his unmasking of Valindin's scheme in the short Second Act. His reliance on intuitive knowledge is fittingly displayed in his rather Unamunian boast to Adriana, as she offers to escort him from the room, that 'conozco el camino mejor que tú. Puedo andarlo sin luz' (519). The analogy thrown up by David's words is a good one. Neither the character nor his creator is suggesting that blindness is somehow preferable to sight, or that intuition can replace rational analysis. We have seen that David is at times led into error. Rather, his words reflect a belief that has become a commonplace of Buero's theatre, namely that the path to progress and change is not necessarily an exclusively rational one. Indeed, many characters and situations in Buero's plays are designed to show that our imagination and intuition can guide us towards the truth more reliably and rapidly than our reason. This is what Feijoo has in mind when he writes that David 'es una encarnación más del mito de Tiresias, la más significative quizás de todo el teatro de Buero' (*20*, p.309). Tiresias, the blind seer of Sophocles's *Oedipus Rex*, is the embodiment of the painful growth through blindness to knowledge. This point is echoed by Juana Salabert in her essay included in the special edition of *El concierto de San Ovidio* published to coincide with the 1986 production:

> Para acceder a la visión simbólica, es decir, a la conciencia que transforma al hombre, es necesario cumplir antes los ritos del paso por la oscuridad, del descenso a los infiernos. (*4*, p.31)

David's blindness, in this way, can be interpreted as an ambivalent symbol of man's complex freedom. He lacks freedom from exploitation at the hands of the sighted (i.e. those in power). But this is compensated for by the fact that as a visionary, blind to the apparent impossibilities which normally surround and forcibly define human life, he possesses the freedom to change, to become. Thus, a seer like Tiresias, he can taunt his companions, '¡Reíd! Siempre habré pensado yo lo que no os atrevíais a pensar. Siempre aprenderé yo cosas que vosotros no os atrevéis a saber' (489). This is the nub of the seer's strength. It is the creative freedom which David attempts to communicate to the other beggars through the potent symbol of the violin. In the broadest of terms, David becomes the persuasive mouthpiece for Buero's own consistent concern to establish hope as the lever which liberates the present from the burdens of the past, and will as the galvanizing element in human nature. David becomes typified by his insistence that 'todo es querer' (491), and this is the most important character trait that he shares with Valentín Haüy. For David, 'querer' is the bridge between the audacious world of his imagination and the world of practical achievement.

The force of his will power will inevitably bring David into open conflict with a whole series of other characters in the play, but before examining the conflictive aspects of his striving character, we should perhaps look at the roots from which his determination grows. We can see at once that, in a very Unamunian way, his 'querer' is a product of his pain, of the frustration that derives from the huge gap between the dynamism of his imagination and the cruelly static system in which he lives. When Donato, rather wonderingly, tells Adriana of David's belief that 'Dios no puede haber querido nuestra ceguera' (514), he is not only describing the older man's divergence from the convictions of the Priora, he is also articulating the great humanistic discovery that man's destiny lies in his own hands. David becomes a sort of Prometheus figure, stealing fire from the gods so that mankind can free itself from the eternal darkness in which it lives. The period in which the play is set assumes a crucial importance in this respect, for it was with the

French Revolution that man began to develop an awareness of his capacity to change the determinant factors of his sociopolitical existence. Divinely ordained authority, as the Priora would understand it, or as Franco claimed to possess it, was successfully challenged, and consciousness of the possibility of change was born. The leading historian A.J.P. Taylor has described the legacy of the French Revolution in similar terms: 'Only from the time of the great French Revolution have there been revolutions that sought not merely to change the rulers, but to transform the entire social and political system.'[28] It is only in this historical framework of political hope which was the positive aftermath of this, the first modern revolution, that we can fully understand Buero's intentions in the depiction of the revolutionary figure of David. As Juana Salabert suggests, David's revolutionary awareness, his 'visión simbólica', implies a constantly painful attempt to transform reality.

It is the perhaps inevitable lot of anyone who stands against the received wisdom of an entire system that he or she will be branded insane. Accordingly, David is held to be 'peor que Gilberto' by his companions (489), and Haüy's outraged intervention during the concert is dismissed as the rantings of a drunkard (552). Once again, it is the figure of Don Quijote which springs to mind. And although David is given no overt quixotic symbolism, unlike others among Buero's canon of visionary characters, there can be no doubt that his capacity to pursue an ideal in the face of widespread disbelief and abuse is a virtue that Buero believes to be the spiritual mainspring of Don Quijote.[29] David's loneliness, at the beginning of the play, is the isolation of the dissenting individual in an inert society. It is the common fate of all of Buero's historical heroes, Esquilache, Velázquez, Goya and Larra, and there can be little doubt that the dramatist senses a similarity with his own situation in the 1950s and 60s. It is a loneliness that David has attempted to assuage, and thereby to keep his imaginative world alive, by the fixation on a

Don Q.

---

[28]*Revolutions and Revolutionaries* (London: Hamish Hamilton, 1980; repr. Oxford: Oxford University Press, 1981), p.17.
[29]For Buero's own dramatic re-working of *Don Quijote*, see his *Mito (Libro para una ópera)* (Madrid: Escelicer, 1968).

sort of Dulcinea figure, Melania de Salignac. An actual historical character who had apparently overcome her blindness, she represents for David a psychological bulwark against the pervasive chorus of disbelief and mockery, and he accordingly surrounds her name with a quixotic devotion: 'sí. Yo creo firmemente que es hermosa' (489). David's need for Melania as a dynamic symbol of possibility is communicated to the audience through his playing of the music from Corelli's *adagio*. But it is Adriana who ultimately leads David from the infinitely rich world of quixotic imagination into the challenge of the real world. David's crucial journey from dream to action is, therefore, paralleled by the creation of a more meaningful set of personal relationships. The psychological truth of Melania is replaced by the real love of Adriana, one based on a shared suffering and poverty, as she herself reminds him:

> Pero supongo que [Melania] será rica ...Sólo así habrá podido aprender lo que sabe. Figúrate, una ciega... Es rica y por eso no es de los tuyos. Ella nunca habrá padecido miedo, o hambre..., como nosotros. (566)

Through Adriana, therefore, David is able to reorient himself more positively in his personal life. And although denied actual children to replace his shattered paternal relationship with Donato, he is at least rewarded with a more worthy spiritual succession in the form of Haüy's pupils.

David's struggle towards the light, therefore, takes place on both a humanistic and an existential level. On one hand, he asserts the basic human right of self-determination. On the other, he breaks free from the world of dream, of pure imagination, into the world of external, physical reality in an attempt to 'desarrollar su personalidad en plenitud', as Cortina puts it (*14*, p.29). This view of David's dual struggle gives us an insight into Buero's account of the personality in the totality of its relationships. Through David Buero depicts the character who is able both to live intensely within himself and to project that inner vitality into the lives of others. The strength of David's inner world enables him to see through and engage in

conflict with Valindin, and his refusal to compromise his principles
is evident throughout. Nowhere is this more clear than in his
relationship with Adriana. Through David's direct intervention in her
life she travels the difficult path from ignorance - 'pero vosotros...
¿amáis?', she heedlessly asks Donato on their first meeting (515)- to
an ability to recognize the blind not as sick animals, but as suffering
subjects in their own right. Like David, Adriana is rewarded with
love, both of them leaving behind the world of casual and self-
interested sex. Without question it is David who stimulates Adriana
into the realization of the possibility of a form of personal plenitude
beyond the self-interest which defines her relationship with
Valindin. Jordan notes:

> If Adriana's relationship with Valindin is basically an
> economic one, regulated by fear and need, the arrival of
> David is enough to widen the already sizeable cracks in
> the patriarchal edifice. (*23*, p.442)

David's inner strength is communicated to Adriana, while her
immersion in the external world enables him to orient himself
emotionally in the pressurized world of real relationships. This
encounter between David and Adriana is immediately suggestive of
a Mary Magdalene/Christ relationship, made explicit at the end of
the play when Adriana calls Donato '¡Judas!' (602). In a sense, any
exemplary figure who moves through a form of passion to
martyrdom will evoke echoes of Christ. But David's emphasis on the
conquering of a new world through faith and power of will, and the
injection of these spiritual values into a world lurching into a
materialistic stagnation, are essentials of the Christology Buero has
embodied in David. The dramatist has himself referred to this as a
conscious intention in the writing of the work:

> En el caso, como puede ser el mío y el de tantos otros, en
> que hayamos dejado de creer en una confesión
> determinada, no por eso dejamos de tener un sedimento
> cristiano muy profundo en cuanto a los valores de

conducta morales y espirituales: y esto se refleja en *El concierto de San Ovidio* porque, en definitiva, aunque de una manera mucho menos mística, David viene a ser una figura que en algunos aspectos recuerda a la de Jesús. Lo cual se utiliza explícitamente en la obra cuando Adriana le llama 'Judas' a Donato. Y no hay doce apóstoles, pero hay unos cuantos ciegos, que podrían ser en alguna medida pésimos apóstoles de un David que no logra tener verdaderos seguidores. Entonces y finalmente, David es sacrificado y ejecutado. Todo esto, claro, tiene una impregnación del cristianismo, que está en efecto conectada con una visión marxista de los conflictos socialtes de la época, y de las reacciones ante ellos. (Inter.)

This dual goal of Marxist analysis and spiritual regeneration, described by Buero in the above words, is perhaps most evident in the play's agitative intention. Like his direct predecessor, Ignacio of *En la ardiente oscuridad*, David can claim a Christlike intent 'a traer guerra y no paz' (36), a burning desire to force others onto the difficult path to knowledge about themselves and about their world. This, of course, brings David into open conflict with many characters in the play, as we have seen. There are specific moments of violence with Elías and Valindin, when David uses his blindman's stick as a deadly accurate weapon, as an 'ojo' as he himself says (572). Although Gagen comments reprovingly on this readiness to aggressive self-defence (*17*, p.47), we must remember that it is both a sign and a direct consequence of a simple but determined refusal to be an object at the mercy of external forces. In fact, the 'garrote' becomes an important dramatic symbol at this point, a clear counterpart of the 'espadín' brandished by Valindin as a symbol of his ascent to privilege. García Lorenzo comments:

Frente a la espada de Valindin, el garrote de David, su ojo - como el ciego afirma - y su defensa, pero también el objeto que acabará con la vida del explotador 'de tres

golpes secos'; un garrote que ha sido señal de auto
afirmación para el ciego y que, arrebatado de su mano
por los dos policías, nos indica que todo está perdido,
que la impotencia de David es ya completa. (*26*, p.111)

But while Valindin's sword denotes a fundamental insecurity ill-
concealed by a display of strength (in that he still feels constrained to
protect his social status by wearing the sword), David's use of the
stick shows how strength can be gleaned from apparent weakness.
Nowhere is this more clear than in the superbly controlled murder
scene when the petulant impotence that Valindin supposes to lie
behind David's 'palos de ciego' (590) is shown to be the final
misjudgment of prejudice.

Throughout the play Valindin constantly underestimates
David's capacity for independent thought and action. The blind
beggar's challenge to paternalistic authority provides a basic model
of relevance to any audience. Whilst Jordan's assertion that David
acts 'in the name of the new liberal humanism' (*23*, p.437) is perhaps
to overstate his degree of political consciousness, it is nonetheless
clear that he is motivated by a coherent system of values which gains
him the sympathy of the modern spectator. Basic among these values
is the humanistic need to 'convencer a los que ven de que somos
hombres como ellos' (489), in general, and, specifically, to cast off
the mask of clown which his involvement in Valindin's enterprise
has forced upon him (590). In this sense, David's struggle is that of
his companions, as Verdú observes:

> El objetivo es esencialmente social: integrar al hombre
> en la humanidad; y el héroe es consciente de la doble
> vertiente que caracteriza la acción emprendida: unir el
> mundo de los ciegos para quebrar el mundo de los
> videntes.(*28*, p.115)

The killing of Valindin becomes, in this light, the 'insurrección de
los oprimidos' (*28*, p.120), an interpretation clearly given added

weight by the close proximity of the incident to the French Revolution itself.

Throughout the play Buero highlights the atrocious sociopolitical conditions of the time, establishing a direct link between that state of mind which could take unguarded pleasure in the 'concierto' and that which heedlessly consumed the lifeblood of the French people. In the epilogue Haüy points to what is a wider historical interpretation of the 'concierto' by calling it 'un ultraje a la humanidad' (603). The outrage perpetrated on David and his companions is but a particularly emotive symbol of the corruption prevalent in a society of 'hambre y ferias' (604). In his conversation with Bernier in the Third Act David realizes the full extent of oppression. His thoughtful '¡cuántas cosas necesitan remedio!' (577) marks his commitment to action, a commitment which reveals Buero's view of the Revolution as a massive popular response to oppression rather than the violent offspring of political pragmatists or ideologues. In a time of 'hunger, nakedness and nightmare oppression,' as Thomas Carlyle has written,[30] Valindin's death, like the Revolution itself, is seen as historical nemesis. In this way, the historical hero provides an unequivocal symbol of a political potential lying deep within the heart of the ordinary people, even those whose capacity for action appears to have been precluded by the most difficult of circumstances. As Doménech reminds us, David 'en el mundo en que vive, es lo *menos* que se puede ser' (*16*, p.215).

But David does not act solely out of social or political motives. There can be no doubt that Valindin's brutal reaction when he finds Donato in Adriana's bedroom, and David's growing involvement with her, are two factors which sharpen the blind man's personal motivation. We have already mentioned that the rebellious David is symbolically rewarded with love. The figure of the rebel who inspires and finds love, at times in the most unlikely of quarters, has become a commonplace of Buero Vallejo's theatre. The basic implication is that human beings, if they are to remain human, must protect the quality of their intimate life whilst still participating in the affairs of the external world. The sense of solidarity that David

[30]*The French Revolution* (London: Bell, 1902), III, 133.

strives to construct with his 'hermanos' (489), the other blind
beggars, must be complemented by a love relationship. Once again,
Buero is stressing the inextricable bond between the personal and the
social in our lives, and showing through the character of David how
these spheres are mutually enriching. David's intelligent courage in
his dealings with the exploitative Valindin wins him the love of
Adriana, whilst her love strengthens his resolve to free himself once
and for all from the impresario's clutches. And as he asserts his own
subjectivity David begins to humanize his perceptions of those
around him. After killing Valindin he is able to recognize that
Valindin was also in love with Adriana. In other words, for the first
time in the play the victim, in the very moment of becoming
executioner, sees his victimiser as a human being with his own set of
problems and desires. This is most clear in the case of his
relationship with Adriana. From despising her as a sexual object
adorning Valindin's private world (prostitute/mistress) and a useful
commodity in his workaday world (waitress), David begins to see
her as a suffering subject in her own right. It is interesting that both
David and Adriana express their aspiration to subjectivity in and
through the motif of music. David begs Lefranc to admit him as 'el
último de los violinistas' in the Opéra Comique (575) and Adriana
refuses to be a waitress in Valindin's café, declaring that 'prefería
cantar y bailar' (495). Faced with the seeming impossibility of their
situation, Adriana and David construct a love relationship in which
they can both assert themselves and yet accept each other at the same
time. The rigid mould of exploiting subject and weakened object is
broken. Although David and Adriana ultimately fail, they at least in
their private world open the way for what Ronald Segal describes as
'the treatment of man with trust and reverence. In the end what the
revolutionary represents is the human promise alive in the very risk
of love'.[31]

An early play, *Casi un cuento de hadas*, is dedicated to the
proposition that the world resolutely refuses to behave as though it
were the setting for an ideal fairy tale. The force of human jealousy
rapidly shatters the idyll of David and Adriana. Ironically, it is

---

[31]*The Struggle against History*, p.132.

Adriana's generous act of self-sacrifice, as she gives herself to Donato, which unleashes most fully the rival passions of the two men. For David, in particular, it is a salutary lesson that the prostitute is no mere object, but rather a suffering human being. This recognition is the first and major step to love. But while David can control his feelings and accept an unpalatable situation for the sake of Donato, as he has already done once before in the final rehearsal for the 'concierto' (545), Donato is a sad victim of his own deep-rooted sexual neurosis (in itself a function of his blindness, as we have seen in other cases). Envy between the two men crystallizes into sudden violence (573) and a corroded relationship. There may well be Oedipal overtones, as Jordan has implied, as Donato, the spiritual son, rebels against the sexual authority of the father (*23*, p.443). It is certainly true that the tension between the human being as subject and as object, a tension that Buero clearly sees as lying at the heart of our political no less than our personal problems, lies also at the heart of the split between David and Donato.

Desperately seeking to assert himself in Adriana's eyes, Donato must attempt to knock David down. He begs him to leave (584) and, later, blinded by jealousy and fear, he betrays him to the police. At the end of the play we infer from Haüy's words that, thirty years after the event, Donato is still obsessed with his treachery. But Cortina is quite wrong to suggest that, like Carlos of *En la ardiente oscuridad*, Donato 'ha quedado impregnado con el aliento de esperanza del hombre de cuya muerte es responsable' (*14*, p.32). He remains locked in a sense of impossibility born of fear and guilt, and his playing of Corelli's *adagio*, rather than a creative echo of David's great imaginative strength, is the hollow voice of obsession, It is his futile atonement. In this way, the Adriana-David-Donato triangle enables Buero to complete his catalogue of obstacles, historical, political and personal, which stand between man and the relatedness he must establish in order to actualize and protect his humanity. It is a triangle which appears in many of Buero's works. In an interview with Angel Fernández-Santos the dramatist notes:

Como recordarás, en casi todas mis obras hay una pareja
masculina con una mujer en medio. Tal vez yo no sea
capaz de contestar con lucidez a una pregunta como ésta,
ya que esta situación que se repite en mi teatro es posible
que esté engarzada a algunas de mis vivencias más
profundas y que, por ello, no sea consciente de todas sus
implicaciones. (*11*, p.75)

This situation reveals, above all, how the external inevitably intrudes
into our intimate lives. In a world of intense pressure David's power
of will, the source of his strength, will lead him into conflict, just as
love, his only possible salvation, will be the ultimate cause of his
downfall. Such is the destructive nexus of circumstances which
Buero pits against his hero.

In this way, through the exemplary story of David, Buero
seeks to break down the separations between the individual and the
general, between private emotion and collective experience and
between humanity and history. The case of Valentín Haüy - and we
should remember that this was the original inspiration for the play -
also shows clearly how a private morality can become a force for
liberation. As Buero's preface to the play indicates, the appearance at
the end of the action of Valentín Haüy is fully integrated into the
meaning of the play. Indeed, it is the very point of the work:

Del Hospicio a la Feria de San Ovidio, que se celebraba
desde aquel año en la que es hoy plaza de la Concordia y
era entonces la plaza de Luis XV, las andanzas de un
grupo de ellos [los ciegos] determinaron sin saberlo el
destino de un gran hombre y motivan esta historia. (474)

Not all critics have been prepared to accept Haüy's epilogue as an
integral part of the play's structure. Both Dixon (*15*, pp.2-3) and
Gagen (*17*, pp.38-39) detail critical reaction to this final scene.
Perhaps most spectacular among the voices of dissent is that of the
anonymous *Times* correspondent who wrote of an Italian production
of the play that 'a somewhat unnecessary narrator appears to speak of

the day when the underprivileged shall achieve equality'. As Gagen remarks, 'needless to say, Haüy is not the narrator, is not unnecessary, and that is not his message' (*17*, p.39).

Valentín Haüy is, in the first instance, the historical survivor of the whole incident, that is the only participant in the affair whose name has been recorded by historians. But of course the drama clearly focuses not on the historical fact but on what we might call the intrahistorical background which gives the fact its full significance for a contemporary audience. The historical play becomes, in this sense, 'el documento de una realidad social pasada', as Pilar de la Puente notes (*27*, p.95). In one way it reveals the impact of specific social structures on individual lives. Beyond this, it highlights the layers of frustration and aspiration, both intimate and collective, which are ignored by the official version of history. In Buero's view it is certainly the purpose of social drama to cast light on the life of ordinary people. But it is also the purpose of an historically based drama, like *El concierto de San Ovidio*, to show that the doors of history are not closed to suffering humanity. This is what Buero means when he writes, in a letter sent to me in November 1977, that the highpoint of rational and civilized historical development will be marked by the ultimate union of intrahistory and history:

> Hay en un indefinido futuro un punto de convergencia (al que quizá niunca lleguemos pero al que sí podemos acercarnos más y más) entre 'intrahistoria' individual (o colectiva) e historia.

The relationship between David and Haüy illustrates this desideratum of Buero's historical thought. Haüy is the ordinary man who, sharing David's sense of outraged humanity, comes to represent the full potential of his people and, entering onto the stage of history itself, is able to transform radically his fellows' existence. In his echo of David's struggle Haüy provides a particularly emotive example of this positive interplay of man and history, of popular aspiration and historical stagnation.

Although critics have been quick to suggest that Haüy's reformist stance is an inadequate response to extreme circumstances, and indeed to some extent represents the continuation of an oppressive paternalism, as we have already seen, it is important to remember that the symbolic act of opening the eyes of the blind to their true potential has overt political (as well as existential) overtones. Rather than defusing a revolutionary situation, as Armando Carlos Isasi Angulo has implied (*15*, p.22), Haüy not only demonstrates a considerable sympathy for the causes which inspired the actual French Revolution (604), but also champions a commitment to a revolutionary change in human attitudes and consciousness. As Dixon notes, Buero's awareness that many revolutions, among them the French Revolution, have been self-defeating because of their tendency to unleash a chain of excessive reaction and counter-reaction leads him to identify personally with Haüy (*15*, p.23). Buero himself has stressed that we live in times in which reform is at least as likely to herald enduring progress as is the violent convulsion of revolution:

> En el estado actual de mi pensamiento, la línea divisoria entre reforma y revolución se va haciendo cada vez más insegura, más fluctuante. Porque, claro, el desarrollo de las sociedades modernas y del mundo en general probablemente está haciendo que la oposición tajante entre lo revolucionario y el concepto de lo reformista se esté dulcificando o suavizando cada vez más. De manera tal que se puede pensar en la posibilidad de una revolución verdadera que, sin embargo, no signifique una convulsión fulminante en una sociedad determinada, sino la consecuencia de toda una serie de reformas agregadas unas a otras, cuya acumulación hace que, en un momento determinado, puede darse el último paso realmente revolucionario, pero mucho menos virulento de lo que podía ser en las revoluciones clásicas. (Inter.)

It is important to note here the emphasis that Buero gives to the idea of a 'revolución verdadera'. Clearly, he is not abandoning his awareness of the need for deep-seated and radical change, nor even a somewhat ambivalent belief, that we have also found in Haüy, that the 'tremenda convulsión' of the French Revolution 'fue mucho más positiva que negativa si la consideramos en su conjunto' (25, p.27). Haüy provides a partial answer at least to Buero's meditation on the possibility of achieving leaps of progress without recourse to violence and crime.

In his poem written during the Spanish Civil War, 'Full Moon at Tierz: Before the Storming of Huesca', the ill-fated English poet John Cornford uses the Hegelian notion of 'qualitative change' to define a moment in history which he felt to have a specific significance for a humanity struggling towards its liberation. His pinpointing of the 'dialectic's point of change'[32] is a reference to the time at which the process of development reaches a point of transition, when a gradual quantitative growth abruptly crystallizes into something new. Hegel uses the image of the child slowly developing in the womb until the moment of qualitative change, that is the birth itself. This transition from foetus to living child illustrates most convincingly the transfer of a growing intrahistorical swell of discontent (embodied by David) onto the platform of history. The past has now ceased to be a dark mass of determining conditions in which man is helpless (the position of the blind beggars at the beginning of the play) and becomes a present moment (the 'presente momento historico' which lies at the centre of Unamuno's *En torno al casticismo*) in which man now has the possibility of exercising choice, of distinguishing between various different directions of development. The humanism of Valentín Haüy marks the birth in history of a new direction for those whose life had been previously hemmed in by a corroding sense of impossibility. Like Cornford just before the battle of Huesca, Buero believes he has located a moment of qualitative change in human affairs. Haüy is a 'gran hombre' because he is the first to help the

---

[32]*The Penguin Book of Spanish Civil War Verse*, ed. Valentine Cunningham (Harmondsworth: Penguin, 1980), pp.130-33.

dispossessed to learn to help themselves. He may very well embody a certain measure of paternalistic guidance, but, nonetheless, his is the vital and truly revolutionary step towards popular emancipation. In the epilogue Buero has Haüy say the following words:

> No es fácil, pero lo estamos logrando. Si se les da tiempo, ellos lo conseguirán, aunque yo haya muerto; ellos lo quieren, y lo lograrán... algún día. (604)

Through his character Buero expresses his own awareness that the future is not an inevitable, necessary development towards freedom, but that it depends upon continued collective struggle. Haüy's new-found belief that progress can be chiselled from the wall of impossibility surrounding the blind beggars by using the tools of human will, effort and decision, immediately recalls David's impassioned pleas to his companions. Dixon notes that Haüy's words echo those 'de un David que también (en poco tiempo) ha envejecido y madurado, pero en quien el dolor de su propio fracaso se acompaña ahora de una fe ardiente en que *otros* triunfarán' (*15*, p.24). Haüy, like David, is an historical hero because he senses that a new world lies within man's potentiality for struggle. History, as *El concierto de San Ovidio* shows, can be not only interpreted by human understanding, but also subordinated to human will. Man's corroding sense of chaos, of impossibility, can be tamed into perspective by the individual imagination. And in the capable hands of a man like Haüy, this dream, deep-rooted in the hearts of many, can become reality, It is for this reason that Buero places the dreamer, especially the pragmatic dreamer like Valentín Haüy, at the centre of his view of history. In other plays of the historical cycle the dreamer is an artist, a writer or a visionary politician. But what they all have in common is the ability to voice the aspirations of the ordinary people, cut off by history itself from any possibility of changing the conditions of their existence. The historical hero, like Haüy, may not be of the people, but he speaks for the people, and his work always marks an important stage in Buero's vision of the conquest of a more just society.

But the historical hero is also characterized by the awareness that human existence is not solely intelligible in historical or political terms. Haüy's final speech is suffused with a sense of the tragedy and pain that, for Buero, are inherent in every individual life. But this, properly speaking, belongs to our final discussion of the speculative aspects of the work, of *El concierto de San Ovidio* as tragedy.

4 *The Tragic Sense of Life*

The fact that *El concierto de San Ovidio* is described by its author as a 'parábola' suggests that it was conceived as a tract for its times. Certainly, the images of poverty, oppression and struggle were particularly valid for Spain in the early 1960s. But more universal values have also emerged in our discussion of the work. On the political level, Buero's analysis moves from a denunciation of authoritarianism to a critique of the defining features of Western capitalism. On the existential level, the work is fired by the passionate belief in the self-determining subject. Human identity is shown to be not static but dynamic. Through the character of David, in particular, we see that human identity is only generated through the active, critical relationship with other subjects. In this way *El concierto de San Ovidio* clearly perceives and illustrates the dialectic between subject and society. It is in this dialectic, as the relationship between David and Adriana makes clear, that the impulses towards freedom lie. But these impulses are opposed by the compulsions, repressions, distortions and sacrifices which are also created by the complexities of intersubjectivity, as the tragic relationship between David and Donato shows.

For the play to function on this level the characters must convince us as individuals. The spectator has to feel drawn into their intimate world, perceiving and sensing there the human complexity of that character's life. If the spectator views the characters as primarily symbols or mouthpieces for the author's political vision, then the work will only rarely transcend the level of didactic or propagandist drama. It is at this point that we can say that *El concierto de San Ovidio* goes beyond the political and historical parable, to become an intense drama of human conflict in which both tension and emotions run high. It is therefore appropriate that Buero himself should have included the play among those works of his which 'quieren ser tragedias' (*17*, p.40). It is a definition echoed by Iglesias Feijoo who describes the play as 'una verdadera tragedia del teatro contemporáneo' (*4*, p.17), and Gagen summarizes it as a 'tragedy of exploitation and a tragedy in the more traditional sense also' (*17*, p.47). This has important implications for the total range of meanings that the play encloses.

In order to understand any play fully we must ask ourselves what sort of reaction the playwright seeks to draw from his audience. It is clear from this discussion that Buero, on one level, seeks to clarify for his spectators the changing political superstructure of the Francoist state, making them aware of both the tremendous restrictions of authoritarianism and the inherent risks of *laissez-faire* market-place economics. But he also creates characters and situations which will involve the audience emotionally with their private destinies. For Buero this latter aspect is a defining element of tragedy. In his essay, 'La tragedia', published in 1958 and in which he expounds his definitive view of tragedy, he notes that 'si ante una obra de tema social de nuestros días el espectador sólo experimenta deseos de actuación inmediata y no se plantea - o siente - con renovada viveza el problema del hombre y de su destino, no es una tragedia lo que está viendo' (*8*, pp.67-68). This is certainly not to be taken as a dismissal of political theatre *per se*. Buero insists that drama whose aim is immediately political can be 'teatro tan efectivo'. but whose framework of reference is necessarily much more limited, 'casi tan fugaz como un cartel publicitario' (*8*, p.670). *El concierto de San Ovidio* belongs to that singular and universal art form, tragedy, which, since the earliest origins of the theatre, has been concerned to depict and understand the suffering that is inevitable in every individual life.

It has been suggested that tragedy as an art form is no longer viable. Living in an era whose most fashionable ideologies - Marxism, Freudianism, Existentialism - are all fundamentally non-tragic, and whose scale of values finds it difficult to cope with tragic grandeur, Buero Vallejo has striven to produce consciously wrought tragedies and has written extensively, more than on any other topic, on his particular tragic vision. In this he is following closely the line of his own national tradition. In his seminal work *El teatro de lo imposible* Jean-Paul Borel characterises Buero, among others, as an inheritor of and contributor to that tradition in Spanish drama which illustrates 'la imposibilidad práctica de vivir lo que se llama "la vida cotidiana" ' (*29*, p.280). Clearly, the tragic sense that arises from this can take many forms. For Benavente, for example, the intimation of impossibility, when not diluted in light comedy, takes the form of a virtually exclusive philosophical concern with the inaccessibility of ultimate truth. For Lorca it springs as a vivid dramatic device from the conceptualized clash between the codified and non-codified impulses of the individual. But for Buero, in an Unamunian way,[33] the tragic sense permeates his very sense of life, the fruit of a profound concern that arises from the individual's conflict with his own limitations, social and metaphysical.

In this way Buero Vallejo's theatre is a plea for both social solidarity and individual integrity, combining a swingeing social critique, deeply rooted in leftist analysis, with a profoundiy humanist concern for the complex, enigmatic existence of the individual *sub specie aeternitatis*. The roots of this double perspective lie in a concrete experience which Buero underwent in the immediate aftermath of the Civil War. In the 'Nota preliminar' which he furnishes to the belated publication of *El terror inmóvil*, a play written in the late 1940s, the dramatist relates how his total political commitment was attacked by a sudden awareness of the agonized uncertainty of individual human destiny. He tells how when in prison he was shown a mysterious photograph of a father cradling a dead child, held so as to seem alive. This photograph was to inspire *El terror inmóvil*, and turned the prisoner's mind to a realm of human experience beyond the immediately political. The quotation is lengthy, but it illuminates a key moment in the development of Buero's tragic vision:

---

[33]For further analysis of this particular aspect of coincidence between Buero and Unamuno, see my article 'The Tragic Sense and its Expression in Unamuno and Buero Vallejo', *Spanish Studies*, 8 (1986), 16-30.

Todos éramos antifascistas; todos estábamos imbuidos de la entereza que nos hacía considerar nuestra quizá cercana extinción como la nada enigmática consecuencia de una noble lucha y de una derrota. Y de repente, ante los ojos, aquel padre bien trajeado, aquel hijo con ropas de primera comunión, venían del pasado a mostrarnos su indiferencia ante las candentes alternativas políticas que habíamos ventilado a fuerza de sangre en España y el indisoluble poso de angustia individual ligada a todo destino humano, poso tantas veces desdeñado por nosotros como un mezquino residuo pequeño-burgués. Pero el residuo se adensaba en la noche silenciosa; mi compañero guardaba aquella foto y yo no la olvidaría. (26)

It is this 'indisoluble poso de angustia individual' which lies at the heart of Buerian tragedy, and which we see forming the nucleus of David's experience of life. The same tension between political endeavour and private destiny which haunted Buero in prison is also established in the play by the final speech of Valentín Haüy. But first we should perhaps reach some sort of understanding of what Buero means when he calls his play a tragedy.

Buero has written enough on his theory of tragedy to leave us in no doubt as to his views. The phrase 'tragedia esperanzada' has become emblematic of his theatre as a whole. There is an apparent contradiction in terms here, which would be held as irreconcilable by those for whom tragedy is always a closed meditation upon human failure. Buero has patiently explained that this is not necessarily so. To be receptive to his ideas on tragedy, to his brand of 'tragedia esperanzada', we must make two preliminary assertions. Firstly, we must accept a necessary distinction between tragedy as a form of theatre and those events and experiences of everyday life that we might call tragic. These two words are often used, virtually indiscriminately, to refer to any sad or painful happening, especially one whose circumstances are particularly shocking. We feel numbed by the impact of these occurrences. Tragedy, as Buero conceives it, is geared as a stimulus to human will, as we shall see. Secondly, and related to a certain extent to this use of the word, we find the term applied to certain works, like Eugene O'Neill's *Long Day's Journey into Night*, which present man as the hapless victim of overwhelming circumstances, unable to do anything other than resign himself to collapse and despair. Such works are unquestionably powerful, but they belong to the pathetic rather than tragic vision. Buero's tragic theatre, and *El concierto de San Ovidio* in particular, is concerned to show how man can react meaningfully with the particular circumstances, historical, political and existential, imposed upon him. The tragic world of Buero is a totally different place from the despairing contemplation of human hopelessness offered to us by the literature of pathos. He notes that 'desde que yo me planteé el problema de lo trágico creí comprender intuitivamente que la tragedia no podía ser una cosa cerrada, sin solución' (*12*, p.222). Perhaps one can detect here, especially in the use of the word 'intuitivamente', an echo of Buero's difficult experiences in prison waiting for his sentence of death to be carried out. Be that as it may, the essence of Buero's theatre is a celebration of what he calls 'la esperanza imbatible del hombre' (*12*, p.224). If he and other writers of his generation write tragedies, it is because 'nosotros llevábamos dentro esa esperanza y escribíamos tragedias, nos diéramos cuenta de ello o no, porque esperábamos, no porque desesperásemos' (*12*, p.224).

In his essay 'La tragedia' Buero justifies this focus on the idea of 'tragedia esperanzada' by reference to the formal construction of Greek tragedy. But he also insists that it is the spirit of tragedy rather than its formalistic elements which he has adapted to his own theatre. For Buero it is this spirit which enables man to humanize his world through the recognition of suffering and through its transcendence. He is fond of summarizing this spirit in the phrase of Beethoven:

> Durch Leiden Freude: por el dolor a la alegría: la más rotunda definición de lo trágico que para mí se ha dado. (*12*, p.224)

This then is the informing spirit of *El concierto de San Ovidio*, a work which seeks to shatter the myth of happiness and spiritual complacency which shroud life, not so as to leave man floundering in despair but to open up the way for a truly human dignity based upon honest recognition and the will to struggle. The theatre, for Buero, is a testing ground in which the spectators confront the pain of existence, and develop resilience from that. In this context Buero's description of 'el pesimismo provisional' of tragedy assumes a crucial importance (*8*, p.75). The spectators are presented with images of extreme anguish of spirit, of loneliness, alienation and guilt. The source of this imagery in *El concierto de San Ovidio* is quite clear, as we shall see at a later point. But in broad terms it springs from the metaphor of blindness, not so much in its political connotations, but in the sense of 'la ceguera involuntaria', the enigmatic uncertainty surrounding human life. Accordingly, David is not just the symbol of struggle. He is also the tragic hero, the blind Tiresias who will open the eyes of the audience. But first, as I commented in the last chapter, the tragic tradition requires that the initiation to knowledge be carried out through pain. Buero clearly intends his spectators both to suffer and to grow with his tragic hero.

Buero has consistently tended to show that tragedy arises from the tension between 'libertad' and 'necesidad' (*8*, pp.68-71), between the freedom which man needs if his life is to have any degree of meaning, and the combination of circumstances which conspires to enslave him to suffering and failure. In this sense, we may clearly perceive that at the start of the play David is yoked to blind necessity itself. His situation provides a perfect symbol of the fundamental loneliness and alienation that has always lain at the heart of the tragic sense, and the struggle that he undertakes during the play has the clear overtones of the tragic hero pitting himself against the enormity of fate. Stressing that 'todos somos ciegos'. Borel insists that 'si Buero Vallejo nos hace participar, durante algunas horas, de la vida de los ciegos, es para que experimentemos nuestra trágica verdad' ((*1*, p.10). When we first meet David the community of which he forms part is one moulded by suffering and fear. If the blind men are 'hermanos', as the Priora reminds them (485), it is as brothers in suffering rather than companions in any worthwhile enterprise. In one way this is a bleak view of the human condition itself, above and beyond the immediate social problems that the character faces. Monleón writes:

> Los personajes se encuentran limitados por los términos de la estructura social en que viven, pero ello no significa que puedan descargar en ella todos sus males. (*11*, p.19)

As I have already suggested in Chapter 2, this tragic sense is heightened by a peculiarly twentieth-century pessimism as to human beings' capacity to effect any change in their circumstances. The French Revolution had witnessed the birth of human possibility, only to have that positive sense eroded and destroyed by the monstrous developments of our century. Presumably this is what Juana Salabert is implying when she quotes Malraux's view that 'nuestro siglo ... ha hecho revivir la vieja noción de fatalidad' (*4*, p.33).

In this way David is in full revolt against both his own 'ceguera involuntaria' and the 'ceguera voluntaria' which makes a hollow mockery of the lives of his companions. Blindness comes to stand for that sense of corroding despair that derives from the suffering inevitable in every human life. But it is also the prime metaphor through which Buero expresses a problem central to the theatre since Ibsen: that is, the extent to which the individual can summon up the necessary moral force to interact with a hostile society. The tragic sense that Buero defines through David pivots on the axis produced by the analysis of timeless human problems as they manifest themselves at a specific moment in time. For Buero, as all his tragedies have made clear, tragedy is not a permanent, unchanging fact. Rather, it refers to a kind of human experience which arises when the individual comes to confront, as he must, the changing conventions and institutions in which his life is set. This is precisely what Buero means when he says that 'lo social nos interesa por cómo repercute en seres concretos de carne y hueso' (*12*, p.222), and his historical theatre as a whole becomes an extended exploration of the intimate problems, changing and unchanging, encountered by individual beings in their existence in history.

David lives shrouded in silence, the social structure which determines his existence killing the possibility of communication. As I have suggested, this loneliness accounts in great part for his prickly attitude towards Adriana. His loneliness makes his relationships brittle, and he becomes self-absorbed in his own tragedy of being blind. His warning to Adriana, '[no] llores ante un ciego' (565), is indicative not only of a sensibility wounded by a deep-rooted frustration, but also of a form of blindness to the suffering of others. When David tells Adriana that each of us is 'como un pozo' (564) he is echoing a fear that is very much of our times, that as our despair and suffering force us to become increasingly private people, we are less and less able to know others deeply enough to establish meaningful relationships. 'Yo estaba solo... Estoy solo' (563), laments David. It is the cry of human beings that tragedy has echoed since the first pieces of Aeschylus. But David is different. His determination to establish a genuine community with his fellows (the orchestra) based on the power of will ('todo es querer') singles him out as exceptional both as a hero in historical terms, and as a human being coping with the timeless problems of despair and isolation. It is this force of will which enables us to identify David, in the first instance, as the tragic hero. Possession of this drive has always been a prime definition of the classical hero, and the first movement of the tragedy is found in the development from will-power to moral force. David, as he steps into the arena of conflict with his blindness, then with Valindin, becomes a potent symbol for the struggle towards liberation.

This struggle against 'necesidad' constitutes the second movement of tragedy in general, and of David's conflict in particular. In the course of this struggle the tragic hero becomes characterized by his moral force, his refusal to compromise. Through his successive responses to the moral dilemma posed by his growing awareness of the reality of Valindin's scheme, and through his rebellion against the painful circumstances in which his life is cast, David grows in stature. Although he becomes progressively isolated from his own community (the influence of Ibsen's *An Enemy of the People* on Buero's theatre is quite clear), David wins the respect of Bernier and, to a lesser extent, Lefranc. But most importantly, as we have seen, he wins the love of Adriana. David has taken an important step in shattering the divisive mould of sighted/blind. Symbolically, he also opens Adriana's eyes, as Doménech remarks:

> el ejemplo de David opera en ella una pronta y radical transformación, hasta el punto de convertir su propia tara, la prostitución, en algo noblemente humano al entregarse al enfermizo y repugnante Donato. (*16*, p.220)

But David is, of course, engaged in a hopelessly unequal struggle against overwhelming odds. Valindin holds all the cards. It is he who holds the purse strings, who controls Adriana's movements and who is legally empowered to obtain writs of indefinite detention. In this sense, clearly, Valindin is the embodiment of 'necesidad', itself as deep-rooted as the urge to freedom. Valindin is as determined to succeed as David, although of course his goals cannot command the approbation of the audience in the same way. When David kills Valindin, therefore, he is acting virtually as a form of nemesis. The audience will empathize with David's action, seeing it, as Doménech has always insisted, as the defence of human dignity itself (*3*, pp.14-17), as an act of human self-assertion in the teeth of impossibility.

When David kills Valindin he reveals not solely an extraordinary degree of awareness, but also an extraordinary capacity for action. It is at this point that we enter the third movement of David's tragedy. At the height of his struggle the tragic hero is forced to act in a way which runs counter to the value system by which he has previously lived. David's entire world is convulsed as a result of his action. His moment of tragic recognition, when he confesses to Adriana that '¡Yo quería ser músico! Y no era más que un asesino' (596), provides one of the most plaintive lines in the whole play. It captures a painful human awareness that nobility of purpose and strength of morality are not enough in themselves, that the individual cannot remain unsullied in the struggle for his precarious freedom. It is important to note that Buero is refusing to glorify David's act of self-assertion, whether we interpret it as reprisal or revolution. If David is left with little alternative other than his violent confrontation with Valindin, he is no less obliged to assume the responsibility for that action.

It is through the character of David that Buero most clearly plays upon his audience's emotional responses. The hope that the spectators may find in David's final drive towards liberation is quite suddenly shattered at the end of the action proper (i.e. before the final appearance of Haüy). Indeed, events at this point in the drama move at a bewildering pace, much more quickly than at any other stage in the play. Let us recall exactly what has taken place. David has murdered Valindin. Secure in the belief that he will not be suspected of the crime - 'No sospecharán. Y de mí menos. ¿Cómo va un ciego a poder matar a un vidente?' (597) - David and Adriana are confessing their mutual love and finalizing plans for their imminent escape from Paris. This scene, forming as it does the passionate climax and resolution of the David/Adriana tension, contrasts in its intimacy with the dramatic tension of the murder scene. We know that David's individual action will not subvert the system which oppresses him and his companions, but it appears at least that it will lead to a new personal freedom found through love. But the slow rhythm of this scene, appropriate to the birth and unfolding of the new union between David and Adriana, is cut across by action taking place simultaneously in the street. The tone of confidentiality is destroyed by the threatening presence of Latouche, dragging the wretched Donato with him. Dramatic tension begins to mount again, at the moment it might perhaps be least expected - or wished for - by the audience. In the space of a couple of stage minutes David has been betrayed, arrested and threatened with torture, Adriana has been left intolerably alone, their new-found love snatched away just at the moment of its birth, and Donato is left with his overwhelming burden of guilt, despised by the woman he too has come to love. The action proper closes on a note of anguish, for characters and audience alike. All seems in vain.

But these images do not constitute the final impression that Buero wants his audience to take from the theatre. His goal is much more positive. In 'La tragedia he writes that 'la tragedia no sólo es temor, sino amor. Y no sólo catástrofe sino victoria' (*8*, p.69). In other words, from the confrontation with pain springs the will to live, and perhaps to change those conditions which have caused the pain in the first instance. In this sense tragedy is affirmative (rather than naively optimistic) because it propounds a whole series of values which seek to show how the ultimate in personal and social disaster can be meaningful. In the tragic world, as it is understood by Buero Vallejo, human action achieves its maximum significance in the struggle man undertakes against powers he can probably not tame, but to which he will not surrender. It is in this way that we may understand Buero's assertion that tragedy is the only genre that faithfully depicts 'la condición humana de la duda y la fe en lucha' (*8*, p.77).

As Gagen suggests, Buero feels very much involved in the debate between optimism and pessimism that has been making itself felt since the beginning of the nineteenth century (*17*, p.41). All tragedy, by Buero's definition, must nourish the tension in the spectator between faith and doubt. If a work is too conciliatory, then the spectators' desire to struggle against circumstances is not engaged. But if the depiction of 'la necesidad' is too powerful, too negative, then their will-power is atrophied and replaced by despair or resignation. This everyday tension between hope and doubt, as we have seen throughout the course of this study, has vital implications both for man's political activity and for the way he orients himself in his intimate world. This then is the overall sense of life that Buero seeks to capture for the stage. All his most successful tragedies are constructed along the axis of this dialectic, this tension between faith and doubt, 'necesidad' and 'libertad'. Some, like *El sueño de la razón*, are closer to the negative pole while others, like *Llegada de los dioses* , may very well be felt to more affirmative, more conciliatory. At all events, Buero's tragedies seek to communicate to the spectator life's tragedy and its possible consolation. How does this apply directly to *El concierto de San Ovidio*?

As I have remarked, the action proper of the work ends on a note of despair for characters and audience alike. It is at this point that Valentín Haüy reappears, not so much to continue the story itself but to enable the audience to understand what they have seen and felt. The word 'understand' is important here, not in the Brechtian meaning of rational analysis, but in the sense of being able to attribute some sort of meaning to what has happened, to find consolation in the midst of apparent impossibility. As Buero has written, 'la tragedia no es necesariamente catástrofe final, sino una especial manera de entender el final, sea feliz o amargo'.[34] It is Valentín Haüy who, in the play's epilogue, will enable the spectator to understand the seeds of victory encased within the galling experience of defeat. In this way the epilogue is a vital facet of the play, both on the level of political parable (an image of change coming about in the fullness of history) and on that of tragedy, in that it fuels the final tension between doubt and hope which, for the tragedian, lies at the heart of our human experience. David's sacrifice is offset by the achievements of Haüy. His words, referring to the blind he is teaching to read, 'ellos lo quieren, y lo lograrán... algún día' (604), remind us that David's central human conviction, 'todo es querer' (491), and aspirations, 'nuestros hijos verán' (599), live on. In this way, Buero offers his audience a deep consolation and profound meaning in an image of the growth of spiritual awareness across the generations, outside the individual life. Something has been achieved and although there is no direct link between the death of David and the work undertaken by Haüy, it is clear that David is felt to survive spiritually in his successor. The spectator, having witnessed the sorry end of David, must console himself with the Kantian reflection that mankind may be perfected as a result of the individual's efforts, although the individual human being himself comes to naught.

These then are the poles between which the play moves. The audience is given images of abandon and death, contrasted with those of spiritual rebirth and achievement. In this way Buero's tragic vision seeks to revitalize the will that he sees as being the crucial element operating our in lives, to prevent it from growing

---

[34]'Comentario', in *La señal que se espera* (Madrid: Escelicer, 1953), p.67.

mechanical and becoming absorbed by either complacency or despair. *El concierto de San Ovidio*, like all tragedies, through its powerful final imagery of human 'libertad' in fruitful conflict with 'necesidad', seeks to stimulate the active hope which Buero sees as the very heart of individual and collective resistance. The audience is being nudged towards a position of new hope, and Haüy's 'lo lograrán' promises historical redress. But tragedy does not seek to escape from the sorrowful contemplation of the enigma of individual existence, from a concern with what one of the characters in *El tragaluz* calls 'la importancia infinita del caso singular' (14). Haüy immediately changes his mood, and that of the audience. The stage direction 'Baja la voz' (604) suggests a switch from the public figure to a more confidential discourse, to the inner man. The tragedy has been resolved on the level of the parable, meaning has been found to compensate for David's death. But all of this takes place on the level of 'la ceguera voluntaria', the human causes of tragedy. For, of course, there is a vital paradox contained within Haüy's final words. The tension between the loneliness and isolation of the individual and the collective enterprise in which he participates, as we have seen at several points in this study, is a profoundly honest recognition of reality. As Dixon suggests, Haüy has learnt that his own individual power of will is subordinate to the collective struggle (15, p.24). But his words end on an ambivalent and intimist note. Beyond the survival and betterment of the species continues the problem of the individual. What happens when we contemplate David's death devoid of all symbolism, outside the parameters of the parable? Haüy poses the crux of the tragedy:

> Es cierto que les estoy abriendo la vida a los niños ciegos que enseño; pero si ahorcaron a uno de aquellos ciegos, ¿quién asume ya esa muerte? ¿Quién la rescata? (605)

The rhythm of life and death, the cyclical view of the rebirth of human potential, is suggested here. But the existence of the individual is finite and, in the absence of any redeeming divinity, its finitude can only be considered with sorrow. On the symbolic level, David's death has been redeemed by Haüy's work. But on the real level, it is an issue we can only consider with awe. The question '¿quién asume ya esa muerte?' is no merely rhetorical pose. The ultimate implication is that we are all responsible, that as we have benefited qualitatively from the turning point in human affairs marked by the revolutionary attitudes of David and Haüy, so we are inextricably linked to them. Speaking about the extent to which the individual must consider himself responsible for what is done in his name, no matter how indirectly, Buero has observed that there can only be one honest conclusion, 'la de que, en el fondo, todos somos, en mayor o menor grado, *coautores de todos los crímenes*. Y la mayor honradez está en comprenderlo e intentar superarlo' (25, p.28). *El concierto de San Ovidio*, in this way, reminds its spectators of their duty to the past. But it also implies that the true way forward lies not in rigid programmes, but in considering these imponderables from an attitude of basic humanity. Haüy continues:

> Ya soy viejo. Cuando no me ve nadie, como ahora,
> gusto de imaginar a veces si no será... la música... la
> única respuesta posible para algunas preguntas. (605)

These, the final words of the play, constitute a half-spoken sentiment whose dramatic strength lies in its poetic nature. We have now left the realm of history and progress to enter into the timeless contemplation of individual destiny and the realization, on the part of the audience, of the appalling discrepancy between the original goals of David and his final fate. 'Cuando no me ve nadie, como ahora' not only confirms that Haüy is not to be taken as a simple narrator, an intermediary between author and spectator, but also highlights the intractable problems, inherent in every individual life, that lie behind the public or historical self. Music in this respect comes to represent the attraction of withdrawal from the struggle for life. In particular, for David, music represented an aesthetic escape from his existence, part of his sensitivity in which he could realize himself in a depth of feeling - it is significant that David, Adriana and Haüy are all lovers of music, in deliberate distinction to Valindin, who confesses his total lack of interest. Music not only confirms these characters' human need for pleasure, but also fulfils a freedom missing from other areas of their experience.

Music is one of man's finest achievements, capable of touching deep in the human psyche, liberating positive emotions that otherwise lie dormant. Indeed, throughout the play, music has stood for the capacity to dream. An appreciation of music, a disinterested surrender of the striving personality to the emotions aroused by music, returns a lost dimension to man. This is, of course, the ultimate goal of *El concierto de San Ovidio* as well. The complex and well-rounded form of the tragedy is for Buero, in a Marcusian way, the prefiguration of a new human harmony.[35] Knowing that the relationship between art and social change is real, but unbearably slow, the dramatist seeks to reawaken the individual's potential for subjectivity, to make him a force and not an object in his world. The effect that music has on David is to be the effect that tragedy has on the audience. In this sense tragedy is inevitably political, as the radical playwright Howard Barker realized in 1986 when he wrote that 'beauty, which is possible only in tragedy, subverts the lie of human squalor which lies at the heart of the new authoritarianism'.[36] In this way the tragic sense expounded by *El concierto de San Ovidio*, concretized for the audience at the end of the play by the music, is a restorative which, in the words of the poet William Blake, 'cleanses the doors of perception to the infinite'. Both music, as Haüy describes it and David experiences it, and tragedy demand a sensitivity to suffering and passion, the growth of imaginative sympathy and the ability to hope and dream. These are also the qualities that are embodied by Buero's historical heroes, personal qualities that Haüy, in particular, transforms and channels into an historical force.

In this way the playwright intends his work to speak to its audience as music does to David and Haüy. On one hand, it is the

---

[35]See Herbert Marcuse, *The Aesthetic Dimension* (London: Macmillan, 1979).
[36]'49 Asides for a Tragic Theatre', *The Guardian* (10 February 1986), 11.

expression and remembrance of painful limitations, a refiguration of destroyed dreams. On the other, it serves to remind us of the inner resources of the human being, in itself a vital political value in the face of benumbing or aggressive socialization. And this is Buero's answer to the central problem of the committed artist, especially one keen to expose the radical limitations imposed upon human existence under Francoism. Herbert Marcuse defines this problem in a series of questions:

> How can art speak the language of a radically different experience, how can it represent the qualitative difference? How can art invoke images and needs of liberation which reach into the depth dimension of human existence, how can it articulate the experience not only of a particular class, but of all the oppressed? (p.40)

In the final analysis, Haüy's words suggest that music, like tragedy itself, refreshes the sensibility of all human beings struggling to develop their own possibilities, enabling them to find consolation and strength in the laborious and at times discouraging struggle that lies ahead. It is this struggle which humanizes the historical process, as we have seen, and in Buero's view man cannot withdraw from that onerous task. But both music and the play also insist that commitment need not entail a neglect of our intimate selves, of the whole problematic business of being a human being. While the action proper of *El concierto de San Ovidio* stresses man's capacity to work out his own social and political destiny, to write his own history, Haüy's speech at the end of the play warns that if action is to retain its human face and if humanity is not to lose itself behind the mask of enterprise, we must always be open to the individual consequences of our actions. While Buero makes clear, through the use of the words 'niños ciegos que enseño', that progress is no mere abstraction, that its benefits are tangible, the tragic sense humanizes us by sensitizing us to the intrahistorical, private consequences of every historical achievement. As Gagen puts it:

What we bear away from the theatre with us is a complex of emotions: perhaps an awareness that the parable has ended optimistically (more or less) while the tragedy has left us with the knowledge that man's struggle for liberation is more problematic than it might at first seem. (*17*, p.50)

Every Buero play is concerned to wring an emotional response from its audience, and Buero himself is clearly a dramatist skilled in manipulating his spectators' feelings. He appears to be fascinated by the stage's possibilities in this respect, and, as I mentioned earlier, this is why he rejects so much of Brechtian theory. He notes that 'en este fascinador juego de lo trágico, si jugamos con pasiones obtendremos pasión' (*8*, p.66). This brings us back to the question posed earlier. What sort of reaction does the dramatist wish to elicit from his audience? For Buero tragedy is the dramatic form which most profoundly moves the spectator, 'es la forma más auténtica para conmover y remover al espectador'.[37] And the root of this emotional response lies in catharsis, the ultimate purpose and effect of tragedy. Accordingly, the meaning of tragedy resides not in the force of what we might call its storyline, but in the effect it produces in the spectator. The whole question is, of course, open to a variety of interpretations, and Buero does scrupulous justice in 'La tragedia' to the complexity of the arguments which the concept of catharsis has provoked. But for reasons of space and clarity of presentation it is probably best to accept and work from Buero's definition. Working from Aristotle's description of the 'purging of pity and fear', Buero writes that the cathartic reaction in the spectator 'no es ya descarga, sino mejora' (*8*, p.67). Catharsis leads through spiritual elevation to an inner perfecting, 'y sólo partiendo de éste cabe hablar de actuaciones concretas de origen catártico' (*8*, p.67).

For Buero, as we have seen, this type of 'actuación' must be accompanied by some measure of taking stock, a marked degree of human awareness and imaginative sympathy. Catharsis is the process through which the individual must pass if his actions are to

---

[37]'Comentario', in *En la ardiente oscuridad* (Madrid: Alfil, 1954), p.90.

retain these vital qualities. One of the most powerful tragedies of the modern theatre is commonly held to be Ibsen's *Ghosts*, deeply tragic in its presentation of the blind force of necessity. In this case it takes the form of congenital syphilis which a son inherits as a result of his father's excesses. The symbolic overtones of this - social, personal and metaphysical - are made clear in the course of the play, as they are in *El concierto de San Ovidio*. But both plays finish with the sombre contemplation of tragedy in the individual life. *Ghosts* ends with the image of Mrs Alving screaming in horror as she prepares to administer a lethal dose of morphine to her insane son. And yet, as Buero is very fond of relating, something very positive came from this disturbing play. As early as 1953 Buero had written an article entitled 'Ibsen and Erlich' in which he relates how Dr Paul Erlich, having been tremendously moved by a performance of *Ghosts* in Vienna, was to devote the rest of his life to the discovery of a cure for that crippling affliction (7). The incident may be apocryphal, as Dixon remarks (26, p.171), but it does illustrate Buero's firm belief in tragedy's capacity to stir the individual into meaningful action, the 'mejora' he refers to in his essay. Moreover, the incident as Buero describes it bears a certain similarity to his later depiction of Valentín Haüy. There can be no doubt that when he first heard of that incident at the fair of St Ovide in the summer of 1771, covered up by history for so long, Buero immediately foresaw the possibilities of creating a character who would embody the same dynamic response to human suffering.

Valentín Haüy presents a fine example of catharsis 'in action' as Buero defines it in these two articles. Within the fictional bounds of the play the character shows how a positive result can derive from apparent hopelessness and brutality (Beethoven's motto comes to mind once again), as indeed the actual event which inspired the play has done. Here we find the undeniable elitism of tragedy, its dependence upon what Buero calls the 'espectador sensible y receptivo' (8, p.68). In similar manner Howard Barker ('49 Asides') has stressed that 'some people want to grow in their souls. But not all people. Consequently, tragedy is elitist'. In the concert scene, however, Valentín Haüy is the ideal spectator (from Buero's point of view), receptive to wider culture ('intérprete') and to the emotional demands of art ('amante de la música'), in sharp distinction to the other patrons of Valindin's café. Haüy's reaction to the degrading events on stage should, one hopes, parallel the reaction of the spectator in the theatre. In any event, those who chose to laugh at the scene should recognize themselves as included among 'aquellos que, sin duda, nunca han sentido las dulces emociones de la sensibilidad' (603). But Haüy's reaction also demonstrates a particular aspect of the process of catharsis which Buero emphasises as being glossed over in Aristotelian theory. He asks why the Greek chooses to emphasise pity and fear:

> ¿Por qué [habla de] estas dos y no de otras, como la ira
> por ejemplo? ¿Es que la tragedia no puede despertar
> nuestra indignación como reflejo de la justa indignación
> de alguno de sus personajes? Sin duda, puede hacerlo...
> (8, p.65)

We can clearly see how pity and fear, the classical components of catharsis, are important factors in Haüy's revulsion - pity for the wretches he sees being humiliated publicly, and fear because he realizes that he himself is caught up in a society whose standards and values are inhuman. But it is anger which lies at the root of Haüy's outburst, anger which drives him to rebel against the spectacle of exploitation, and anger which dynamizes his whole life. The confrontation with suffering and the sudden awareness of the degrading nature of the society in which he lives lead him to search for a meaning both for himself and for those who have suffered injustice and humiliation. In this sense, Haüy cannot be considered by any standard a tragic hero. Nor is he a revolutionary. He is, however, like Paul Ehrlich, the ideal spectator who will incorporate the willpower, strength and awareness he gleans from his sudden confrontation with adversity into action for others. In doing so, he will enrich his own existence.

As I mentioned earlier, there is no direct link between Haüy and David. Yet it is David who asks anxiously from the stage what it is that Haüy has shouted, and to whom Haüy repeats his damning indictment of a society sunk in frivolous and hypocritical diversion, '¡He dicho que si viérais, el público sería otro espectáculo para vosotros!' (552). But apart from their link as actor and ideal spectator in a particular human tragedy, they are united by a common power of will which is the fruit of anger. Their acts of revolt are prompted by anger at the unpalatable reality of injustice, and specifically at an image of human suffering caused by the indifference of other human beings, above and beyond the suffering inherent in the human condition. Haüy's 'fuerte puñetazo' (551) on the table is a direct dramatic equivalent of David's use of his blindman's stick. It is the rage of the 'mozo exaltado', as Haüy himself puts it at the end of the play (603). Anger and youth are for Buero a vital combination, in which dissatisfaction with the present merges with future potential. And let us recall that in 1962 we are still in the era of the angry young men who had exploded onto the British scene a few years earlier.

This idea of anger is an appropriate point of departure in our discussion of how Buero conceives, and *El concierto de San Ovidio* illustrates, the relationship between tragedy and society. It will be clear from what has been said before that while Buero sees tragedy as enriching man's spiritual world, he sees no less clearly that the confrontation with tragedy galvanizes man's and society's capacity for meaningful action. In other words, Buero has turned to the writing of tragedy partly from his own experiences during the dark formative years of the Civil War and its aftermath, partly because he sees it as the most suitable art form for a world sinking into inertia. He refers to this potential of his art, obliquely as he must, in the essay of 1958. The basic idea contained here is that through the honest confrontation with pain, almost as a biological law, man grows within himself and within his relationships with others:

> La mayoría de edad mental y sentimental sólo puede adquirirse por el avezamiento y no por la huida, lo mismo que la resistencia al dolor físico. La evitación del

error sólo puede conseguirse por el conocimiento del
error y no por la ignorancia. (8, p.78)

To couch it in the terms of the central metaphor of Buero's theatre,
people's eyes are opened through the experience of pain, even
vicariously through drama:

> Si los hombres no ciegan del todo, seguirán sacando de
> la tragedia preciosas enseñanzas que les servirán... (8,
> p.87)

A form which stimulates pain and yet dares to search for meaning
beyond the pain barrier can prepare the ground for a new
consciousness. In a society animated by a shallow, dishonest
optimism, and which demands increasing uniformity of its members,
Buero's immediate goal is to return to the individual his right to feel
pain, to break down the false links between human beings so that in
the honest recognition of our own pain and that of others, a genuine
community may be formed. Barker, whose attempt to define a new
working tragedy for the British stage, from which it has been so long
absent, bears a remarkable theoretical similarity to what Buero has
actually been doing for nearly forty years, affirms that 'in the endless
drizzle of false collectivity, tragedy restores pain to the individual'.
The complexity of the tragic vision, in the able hands of a writer like
Buero Vallejo, can become a vital source of resistance to the empty
optimism which cuts the heart from human life. Human beings
become united by their humanity and not by surface similarities. We
have then arrived at a new and more humane form of looking at
other people. Buero observes that human beings are more united
than is at first apparent:

> In fact, the most common circumstances of our time -
> doubt and distress - already form, although in a
> subterranean and inorganic way, an enormous public,
> inwardly united before the literary manifestation of
> tragic order; it is a collectivity without name which
> perhaps tomorrow, if we arrive at a fuller and more

harmonious form of social life, will transform into that organic collectivity which will fervently support a socially representative tragic stage. [38]

The phrase 'collectivity without name' is immediately suggestive of the intrahistorical depths of national life, the existence of all the 'hombres oscuros' like Valentín Haüy and David. In this way, *El concierto de San Ovidio*, as a socially representative tragedy, provides an image of the growth into self-awareness of human beings who previously had been little more than objects, prevented from establishing any meaningful relationship with their fellows by a system which insists on constantly subverting individual needs to considerations of profit or of ideology. Centrally concerned with justice and the need to re-define the parameters of human freedom, *El concierto de San Ovidio* is a passionate attempt to enable that nameless collectivity to begin to assert itself, to demand a name in that 'fuller and more harmonious form of social life', the driving hope in all of the plays of Buero Vallejo.

---

[38]'Antonio Buero Vallejo answers Seven Questions', *Theatre Annual*, 19 (1962), 1-6.

Bibliographical Note

Buero's work has always attracted a great deal of attention, both in academic circles and, in Spain, in the popular press. But, over the last twenty years especially, interest has been growing steadily. This bibliography makes no claim to be anything like exhaustive. It limits itself instead to the most influential studies and to those which are most readily obtainable.

A. CRITICAL EDITIONS OF 'EL CONCIERTO DE SAN OVIDIO'

1. *El concierto de San Ovidio*, with an introduction by Jean-Paul Borel, Colección Voz-Imagen (Barcelona: Aymá, 1963). Concentrates on the strong moral substance of Buero's work.
2. *El concierto de San Ovidio, El tragaluz*, ed. Ricardo Doménech, Clásicos Castalia, 35 (Madrid: Castalia, 1971). A comprehensive introduction together with useful notes.
3. *El concierto de San Ovidio*, ed. David Johnston, Colección Austral, 82 (Madrid, Espasa Calpe, 1989).
4. *El concierto de San Ovidio*, in a special issue of *Primer Acto*, 38 (1962). Contains important articles on both play and author by Carlos Muñiz, Gonzalo Torrente Ballester, Ricardo Doménech and José Monleón.
5. *El concierto de San Ovidio* (Madrid: Teatro Español, 1986). Souvenir edition of play published to coincide with Miguel Narros's production in the Teatro Español. Includes several interesting articles, in addition to production notes and some memorable photographs.
6. *El concierto de San Ovidio*, ed. Pedro N. Trakas (New York: Charles Scribner's Sons, 1965). A comprehensive student edition. The edition contains a factual and straightforward introduction by Juan R. Castellano.
7. Teatro Español 1962-63, ed. Pedro Saínz de Robles (Madrid: Aguilar, 1964). A selection of the best plays of the season. The book reproduces several of the first-night reviews.

B. OTHER WORKS BY BUERO

8. 'Ibsen y Ehrlich', *Informaciones* (4 April 1953). An early piece in which Buero sets out his theory of catharsis leading to considered and meaningful action.

9. 'La tragedia', in *El Teatro: enciclopedia del arte escénico*, ed. Guillermo Díaz-Plaja (Barcelona: Noguer, 1958), pp.63-87. Essential reading for anyone seriously interested in coming to terms with Buero's view of tragedy.

10. 'Antonio Buero Vallejo habla de Unamuno', *Primer Acto*, 59 (1964), 19-21. A lecture, given by Buero as part of the centenary celebrations of Unamuno's birth, in which the dramatist describes him as forming part of a vital and continuing radical tradition in Spanish literature. Casts a great deal of light on the way that Buero clearly views his own work.

11. 'Del Quijotismo al "mito" de los platillos volantes', *Primer Acto*, 100-01 (1968), 73-74. The intriguing title refers to *Mito*, Buero's only opera, in which a contemporary Don Quixote figure pins his faith on the imminent arrival of saviours from Mars. The article provides important insights into quixotism, one of the central myths in Buero's theatre.

12. *Teatro*, Colección El Mirlo Blanco,10 (Madrid: Taurus, 1968). Contains *Hoy es fiesta*, *Las Meninas* and *El tragaluz*, as well as important critical essays (notably by José Monleón) and several short pieces by Buero himself.

13. 'De mi teatro', *Romanistisches Jahrbuch*, 30 (1979), 217-27. An analysis of Buero's own brand of socially responsive tragedy. Also has interesting things to say about some of the 'defectos premeditados' of various works, including *El concierto de San Ovidio*.

14. 'Una fe llena de dudas', *La Calle*, no, 180 (1981), 47-49. Wide-ranging interview in which Buero talks candidly about the role of the Church and the development of post-Franco Spain.

C. STUDIES ON BUERO

15. José Ramón Cortina, *El arte dramático de Antonio Buero Vallejo* (Madrid: Gredos, 1969). A basic introduction to the first twenty years of Buero's theatre. The analysis is essentially thematic.

16. Victor Dixon, ' "Pero todo partió de allí...": *El concierto de San Ovidio* a través del prisma de su epílogo'. Lecture given in the Teatro Español, Madrid, as part of a cycle of talks on Buero's theatre held to coincide with the Narros production. Thoroughly comprehensive analysis of Valentín Haüy, stressing the central importance of the epilogue in any

attempt to understand the play fully. I am particularly grateful to Victor
Dixon for furnishing me with a copy of his talk before its publication.

17. Ricardo Doménech, *El teatro de Buero Vallejo: una meditación
     española* (Madrid: Gredos, 1973). Broadly chronological study of the
     principal ideas and techniques of Buero's theatre. The final chapter,
     which emphasizes the unity and sense of coherence that Buero's work
     has maintained in spite of clear changes of direction over the years, is
     of particular note. In terms of *El concierto de San Ovidio*, however, the
     book adds little to what Doménech has said in 2 and 3.

18. Derek Gagen, 'The Germ of Tragedy: The Genesis and Structure of
     Buero Vallejo's *El concierto de San Ovidio*', *Quinquereme*, 8 (1985),
     37-52. Comprehensive account of the part played by Valentín Haüy in
     both the inspiration and structure of the play. Particularly good for
     secondary sources.

19. Carmen González-Cobos Dávila, *Antonio Buero Vallejo: el hombre y
     su obra* (Salamanca: Universidad, 1979). As the title suggests, contains
     a good deal of biographical information. The analysis of *El concierto
     de San Ovidio* stresses the conflictive relationship between the
     individual and society.

20. Martha Halsey, *Antonio Buero Vallejo*, Twaynes World Authors Series,
     260 (New York: Twayne, 1973). Basic introduction to Buero's theatre,
     written in English.

21. Luis Iglesias Feijoo, *La trayectoria dramática de Antonio Buero
     Vallejo* (Santiago de Compostela: Universidad, 1982). The most
     substantial study to date on Buero's theatre. All of the plays are tackled
     intelligently, and related to an overall vision of the shifting tones and
     balances that have made themselves felt in Buero's theatre over the
     years. The chapter on *El concierto de San Ovidio* is highly
     recommended.

22. David Johnston, '*El Concierto de San Ovidio*: The Struggle against
     History', *Journal of the Modern Language Association of Northern
     Ireland*, 4 (1980), 1-8. Concentrates on the play as a parable of
     historical hope.

23. -, 'Posibles paralelos entre la obra de Unamuno y el teatro "histórico" de
     Buero Vallejo', *Cuadernos Hispanoamericanos*, no. 386 (1982), 340-
     66.

24. Barry Jordan, 'Patriarchy, Sexuality and Oedipal Conflict in Buero
     Vallejo's *El concierto de San Ovidio*,' *Modern Drama*, 28 (1985), 431-
     50. A sophisticated analysis of the play in terms of its exposition of
     sexual oppression as a function of a more broad-based economic
     exploitation.

25. Robert L. Nicholas, *The Tragic Stages of Antonio Buero Vallejo*
     (Chapel Hill: Estudios de Hispanófila, 1972). Attempts to deal with the
     technical rather than the purely thematic aspects of Buero's theatre. The

chapter of *El concierto de San Ovidio* analyses the play in terms of what Nicholas identifies as its essentially musical structure.

26. Patricia W. O'Connor and Anthony M. Pasquariello, ed., *Buero Vallejo: el hombre y la obra (homenaje a Antonio Buero Vallejo en Nueva York), Estreno,* 5 (1979). This special issue of *Estreno* contains a three-part survey of Buero's theatre written by Martha Halsey, John W. Kronik and Francisco Ruiz Ramón, in addition to other critical articles and several interesting pieces by Buero himself.

27. Mariano de Paco, ed., *Estudios sobre Buero Vallejo,* Los Trabajos de la Cátedra de Teatro, 2 (Murcia: 1984). Reprints some of the most important critical studies on Buero's theatre.

28. Pilar de la Puente, 'El teatro histórico de Buero Vallejo', *El Urogallo,* 2 (1970), 90-95. Deals well with the dialetical relationship between past and present in *Un soñador para un pueblo, Las Meninas* and *El sueño de la razón.*

29. Joaquín Verdú de Gregorio, *La luz y la oscuridad en el teatro de Buero Vallejo* (Barcelona: Ariel, 1977). An intelligent and readable study of Buero's theatre in and through the dominant metaphor of light/darkness. The chapter on *El concierto de San Ovidio* contains many important insights.

D. GENERAL VIEWS OF THE MODERN SPANISH STAGE

30. Jean-Paul Borel, *El teatro de lo imposible* (Madrid: Guadarrama, 1966). Locates Buero's tragic sense in the awareness of impossibility that lies at the heart of his philosophy of history.

31. Ignacio Elizalde, *Temas y tendencias del teatro actual* (Madrid: Cupsa, 1977). Situates Buero's work in a broad European framework, although analysis of the individual plays is not particularly incisive.

32. María Pilar Pérez-Stansfield, *Direcciones del teatro español de posguerra* (Madrid: Porrúa Turanzas, 1983). One of the best of the recent crop of surveys of the modern Spanish theatre. The section which deals with the innovative aspects of Buero's historical theatre is of particular note.

33. Francisco Ruiz Ramón, *Historia del teatro español: siglo XX* (Madrid: Alianza, 1971). Includes an important survey of Buero's theatre in terms of its commitment to searching out the truth about man and his society.

CRITICAL GUIDES TO SPANISH TEXTS

Edited by
J.E. Varey and A.D. Deyermond